Sweet Surprises
for the
Holidays

by
Mella Weeks Bedell and Alisa Bangerter

Illustrated by
Shawna Muchmore

Gingerbread Garden, LLC

Acknowledgement

We wish to express special thanks to our husbands, Dan Bedell and Tim Bangerter, for their endless patience, love, and support.

Shawna Muchmore has spent many hours drawing the wonderful illustrations for this book. We appreciate her sharing her creative talent. We also wish to express appreciation to Tadd Peterson for his graphic design work on the cover.

Many, many thanks to all of our friends and family members who have shared ideas and have encouraged us to create this book.

Gingerbread Garden, LLC
P.O. Box 1213
Centerville, UT 84014-5213

Printed in the United States of America
10 9 8 7 6 5 4 3 2

Library of Congress Catalog Card Number: 97-73819
ISBN 0-9659101-0-5

Notice: The information contained in this book is true, complete, and accurate to the best of our knowledge. All recommendations and suggestions are made without any guarantees on the part of the authors or publisher. The authors and publisher disclaim all liability incurred in connection with the use of this information.

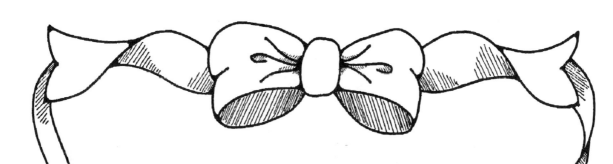

TABLE OF CONTENTS

INTRODUCTION

Many lifetime memories center around the magical atmosphere of holiday celebrations. What heart isn't warmed by the memory of melt-in-your-mouth, chocolate-covered marshmallow eggs, the sight of a glowing jack-o'-lantern, or the spicy smell of gingerbread? Holidays bring friends and families together and provide opportunities for unforgettable experiences.

At the request of many, we have written *Sweet Surprises for the Holidays* as a guide to help you create fun-filled memories and traditions throughout the year. This book is filled with a variety of ideas that we have created and collected over many years. Whether you need a unique recipe, a party game, a table decorating idea, or a simple gift, you will find the perfect idea inside! You will also find family traditions, holiday tips, and many activities that are fun for all ages. Use and adapt these ideas to let holiday magic permeate your home.

MAY ALL YOUR HOLIDAYS BE FILLED WITH SWEET SURPRISES

Mella and Alisa

Try this practical tip to help organize favorite holiday recipes. Color-code recipes by placing Valentine's Day recipes on pink cards, Easter on lavender, Halloween on orange, Christmas on red, etc. Color-coding will help you find holiday recipes quickly at a glance.

CONFETTI BAGS

- *Pop these confetti filled bags at the stroke of midnight.*

Confetti bags are fun and simple to make. If you are having a New Year's Eve party, make confetti bags for each guest or have guests join in the fun by making their own bags. Decorate paper lunch bags with markers, stickers, glitter, etc. Fill bags 1/3 full with brightly colored purchased confetti. Homemade confetti can also be made by cutting paper into small pieces or by using a paper punch. Blow air into bag to inflate. Tie inflated bag closed with ribbon or string. As midnight approaches give everyone at least one confetti bag to pop. The air will be filled with confetti!

CONFETTI CEILING

- *Pop these balloons at midnight to release confetti!*

Fill colorful balloons with paper or metallic confetti before blowing them up. Stretch neck of balloon over the end of a funnel for easy filling. Blow up balloons and tie a long ribbon on each balloon. Hang confetti filled balloons from the ceiling by the ribbons so they hang just above the heads of the party guests. As midnight approaches, give everyone a pin and let them pop the balloons at the stroke of twelve. Confetti flies about!

FAMILY TIME CAPSULE

- *Make some future memories.*

Make a time capsule involving each family member. Have each person write down goals, likes and dislikes, and fun facts about themselves. Young children may wish to draw a picture. Place items in a box and tape box shut. As a family, decide when to open the box. Write instructions on the box for when it should be opened and store in a secure place. Five or ten years may be a good choice, or open a time capsule each year on New Year's Eve. A fun and revealing project.

NEW YEAR'S NOISE MAKERS

- *Homemade noise makers for bringing in the new year!*

Want to celebrate at midnight? Make some noise! Make simple inexpensive noise makers from items commonly found around the home.   Try some of the following:

Sandpaper Blocks – Attach sandpaper to two wooden blocks and rub together.
Bongo Drum – Cut a circle from an old inner tube and stretch it over the opening of a large round can. Secure inner tube around can with an elastic or heavy duty string. Slap drum with open hands or two wooden spoons.
Shaker – Fill a clean, empty, plastic soda bottle 1/3 full with dry beans or popcorn kernels. Replace lid and shake.
Rattler – Staple two paper plates together along edges leaving a small opening. Place 1/2 cup dry beans or dry macaroni into the "pocket" and staple closed. Decorate with markers or stickers and staple streamers around the edge. Shake like a tambourine.
Pots and Pans – Use pots, pans, and lids to make a joyful noise. Simply hit the pots and pans with a wooden spoon or clang the lids together like cymbals.
Bells – String bells on a strong thread or cord and shake away.
Musical Glasses – Fill drinking glasses with different amounts of water. Hit glasses gently with a spoon or a knife for a fun xylophone.

CASCARONES

- *Decorated eggshells filled with confetti make great party favors.*

Cascarones are eggshells filled with confetti and are popular in Mexico and Spain.

Carefully break a small hole in one end of a raw egg. Gently shake out the contents of the egg and discard.   Rinse and drain empty shells. Eggshells can be colored with egg dye and decorated with glitter if desired. Let dry well.

Fill shells about 3/4 full with purchased confetti, or cut newspaper into tiny squares to fill shells. Cover the hole in the eggshell with a piece of masking tape.

Throw cascarones at midnight to fill the room with confetti.

Cascarones can also be inserted into a festive **paper wand**. To make a wand, roll two sheets of newsprint (10" x 12") into a tight cone and glue to secure. Make sure confetti-filled egg can fit into the opening of the cone and glue it in place. Wrap and glue pieces of brightly colored tissue paper around newspaper wand to decorate. Tissue paper can be cut into fringe, or paper "petals" can be made around the egg by cutting tissue into large scallops and gluing into place.   Add pieces of curling ribbon to the end of the cone to make a long tail. "Bonk" these on the heads of friends and family to release the confetti from the eggs.

NEW YEAR'S HAT CONTEST

- *Have each party guest create a one-of-a-kind New Year's hat.*

While waiting for the New Year to arrive, have a hat making contest with all your party guests. Provide guests with plain paper hats (available at party supply stores), or cardstock, scissors, and glue to create their own. Have a variety of items available that can be used to decorate the hats such as glitter, beads, sequins, feathers, pom-poms, fake jewels, felt, tinsel, confetti, small clocks, etc. During the evening judge the hats and give out prizes. Give prizes for the most silly, most festive, most creative, etc.

FISHING FOR PROFESSIONS

- *A fun game for younger children or teenagers to "catch" their future profession.*

Use a blanket or large piece of cardboard to make a screen to throw a fishing line over. Make fishing poles by using a dowel with yarn attached. Tie a clothespin on the end of the yarn. Have each person take turns throwing his/her line over the blanket. Someone sitting on the other side of the blanket attaches an item to the clothespin. The person "fishing" takes the item caught and compares the item to a previously prepared chart on the wall. The chart will identify future professions. Use the following ideas or create your own.

Nail – Carpenter	Comb – Beautician/Barber
Adhesive bandage – Nurse	Surgical glove – Doctor
Toothbrush – Dentist	Bag of coins – Banker
Flag – Politician	Wooden spoon – Chef
Paintbrush – Artist/Painter	Package of seeds – Gardner
Small toy car – Race car driver	Screwdriver – Mechanic
Light bulb – Electrician	Toy airplane – Pilot

A twist on this idea could be to have each item represent a fortune instead of a profession. Some examples are: coins - money in the future, comb - new hairstyle, adhesive bandage - good health, treasure map - exciting adventure, small toy plane - travel, toothbrush - no cavities, etc. Be creative! The possibilities are endless.

FIND THE TIME

- *The team that finds the most time wins.*

Write different time amounts (20 minutes, 1 1/2 hours, etc.) on numerous cards or small paper clocks. Hide the papers throughout the house. Divide party guests or family members into two teams. Tell each team that time is lost and must be found. The teams search for the hidden cards. When all the cards have been found, the time from each card is added together and the team with the most "time" wins.

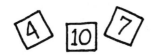 

NUMBER GAME

- *Stand on numbers to win prizes.*

Write the numbers 1 through 12 (to represent the numbers on a clock) on squares of paper and laminate if desired. Randomly tape numbers onto the floor of the room. At the stroke of each half hour or on the hour, ring a bell and party guests must find a number and stand on it. Only 1 person can stand on each number at a time, so only 12 people will be eligible for the prize each time the bell rings. Draw one of the corresponding numbers from a bowl and the person standing on that number wins a prize. At midnight the lucky person standing on number 12 wins the grand prize

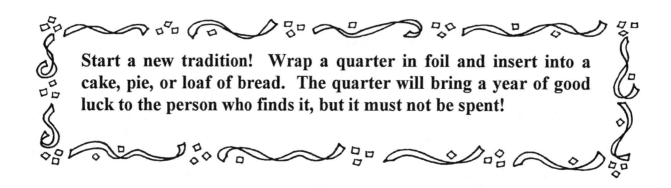

Start a new tradition! Wrap a quarter in foil and insert into a cake, pie, or loaf of bread. The quarter will bring a year of good luck to the person who finds it, but it must not be spent!

FORTUNE PUNCH

- *Macaroni letters found in glasses of punch reveal fortunes for the coming year.*

Make your favorite punch or beverage to serve at a New Year's Eve party. Before serving the beverage, sort one of each letter of the alphabet from a bag of macaroni letters. Drop one letter in each glass and fill with beverage. Serve. After guests have finished drinking their beverages, the letters will be at the bottom of their glasses. Guests can find a fortune for the new year by comparing their letter to the corresponding letter on a chart you have previously prepared (see below). You may wish to change some of the fortunes to fit the guests at your party.

A – Airplane trip
B – Better opportunities
C – Cold cash
D – Dreams fulfilled
E – Extra energy
F – Family fun
G – Good luck
H – Health
I – Increased wealth
J – Job advancement
K – Kick a bad habit
L – Lots of love
M – Movie career

N – New car
O – Oodles of fun
P – Peace of mind
Q – Quick success
R – Romance
S – Surprise in future
T – Travel abroad
U – Uncle coming
V – Vacation
W – Wild adventure
X – Excellent job
Y – Year of bliss
Z – Zest for life

NEW YEAR'S TABLE DECORATING IDEAS

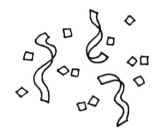

- *Decorate a festive table to celebrate the new year!*

Colorful Confetti Table
For a quick and easy decorating idea, sprinkle table with confetti. Place streamer confetti down the center of the table or use a lot of curling ribbon. Tiny plastic clocks placed among the confetti add a finishing touch.

Cookie Confetti
Make your favorite sugar cookie dough and separate into several portions. Color each portion of dough by kneading in food coloring. Roll out to approximately 1/4" thick and cut shapes with tiny cookie cutters. Irregular shapes can also be cut with a knife or pizza cutter. Place the shapes onto a cookie sheet and bake at 350 degrees for about 5-6 minutes or until bottoms are slightly brown. Let cool. Sprinkle this colorful, edible confetti down the center of the tables and let guests munch away.

Sparkling Cider Centerpieces
Purchase several bottles of non-alcoholic sparkling cider. Wrap each bottle with brightly colored cellophane, gather at the neck, and tie with curls of ribbon. Attach a helium balloon to the bottle if desired. Place the decorated bottles on a buffet table or use as a centerpiece at each dinner table. Guests can pour their own drinks from the centerpiece as needed.

Party Glasses
Decorate clear plastic drinking glasses with glitter paint, small stickers, jewels, etc. Write the name of each guest on a glass. Glasses look festive and add a personal touch to the party.

Filled Favors
Fill empty toilet tissue rolls with small toys, candy, or other small items to be used as favors. Wrap the filled rolls with brightly colored tissue paper or crepe paper allowing the paper to hang over each end 2 1/2". Twist the paper at each end to close and tie shut with ribbons. Decorate outside of tube with glitter, beads, stickers, etc. Use as a favor at each place setting or fill a basket with the favors and give one to each guest as they leave the party.

New Year's Napkins
Tie paper or cloth napkins with curling ribbon or streamer confetti. Napkins can also be placed through paper horns with the blowing end cut off.

Disposable Tablecloth
Cover table with butcher paper and using a 2" square sponge and acrylic paints, randomly sponge-paint colorful squares over paper. Use several colors of paint. Paint can also be splattered on the paper.

Midnight Alarms
Purchase inexpensive alarm clocks in bright colors. Set clocks so all alarms will ring at the stroke of midnight. Place clocks around the house or use as centerpieces on a table and sprinkle confetti, party hats, or noisemakers among the clocks. Have each guest take home a clock as a party favor.

FORTUNE COOKIES

- *A prediction for the new year!*

  1/2 c. flour
  1/4 c. granulated sugar
  2 Tbs. cornstarch
  1/2 tsp. salt
  1/4 c. vegetable oil
  2 egg whites
  1/4 c. water

Cut small strips of paper and write a fortune or message on each strip. Set aside. Mix dry ingredients together and stir in oil, egg whites, and water. If necessary stir in more water to make a thin batter. (Food coloring can be added to batter for colored cookies.) Lightly grease a non-stick griddle. Set heat at 350 degrees. Pour one small spoonful of batter onto hot griddle and quickly smear batter around with the back of the spoon to form a 3" circle. Cook until golden brown. Turn cookie over and cook for a few more seconds. Remove from heat, place a fortune in center of cookie, and quickly fold in half until edges meet. Grasp each corner and pull down together so they meet and form a fortune cookie shape. Place each cookie in a muffin tin cup to cool. Makes about 50 cookies.

FESTIVE FIZZ

- *Make a midnight toast with this beverage.*

  2 pkg. unsweetened powdered drink mix
    (any flavor)
  2 c. granulated sugar
  2 qts. water
  1 can (46 oz.) pineapple juice
  2 qts. ginger ale
  1/2 gallon sherbet (opt.)

Mix powdered drink mix, sugar, and water. Add pineapple juice and chill. Add cold ginger ale when ready to serve. For a frothy beverage, add sherbet to punch. Use raspberry flavored sherbet with red punch and pineapple flavored sherbet with green punch.

PARTY CONES

- *Edges of these ice cream cones are dipped in chocolate and candy sprinkles.*

Dip the rims of sugar or waffle ice cream cones into melted chocolate, coating the cone about 1/2" down. Immediately dip in brightly colored candy sprinkles or in chopped nuts. Let chocolate set and then fill cone with scoops of your favorite ice cream or frozen yogurt.

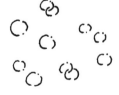

SPARKLING PARTY PUNCH

- *A fun way to serve soda.*

Freeze brightly colored fruit juices or flavored punch in separate ice cube trays. Be sure to have a variety of colors. Allow guests to fill their glasses with the choice of colored ice cubes. Finish filling glasses with clear lemon-lime soda. As the flavored ice cubes begin to melt the soda will gradually become colored and flavored. *Note:* If mixing flavored ice cubes, make sure flavors will complement each other.

MIDNIGHT SNACKS

- *Fill platters with these quick and simple treats for your guests to enjoy!*

Ham Rolls
Purchase thinly sliced ham from a deli. Make or purchase potato salad. Place a small amount of potato salad on each ham slice and roll up. Secure with a fancy party toothpick.

Stuffed Mushrooms
Purchase 50 large mushrooms. Wash and remove stems. Place mushroom caps on a cookie sheet. Add 1 cup chopped mushroom stems (more if desired) to 1 pound of ground sausage. Brown sausage and chopped mushrooms and drain. Mix sausage mixture with an 8 ounce package of cream cheese. Spoon mixture into the mushroom caps. Bake at 325 degrees for 8-10 minutes until hot or place under broiler for 5 minutes.

Tortilla Roll-Ups
Mix together softened cream cheese with dry ranch-flavored salad dressing mix to taste. Spread flour tortillas with cream cheese mixture. Sprinkle chopped green chilis, red pimentos, and chopped olives onto the cream cheese. Roll up tightly and refrigerate for at least one hour. Slice into 1/2" slices to serve.

Water Chestnut Bacon Bites
Drain a can (5 oz.) of water chestnuts. Place water chestnuts in a small bowl and cover with soy sauce. Marinate for 20 minutes. Drain chestnuts and discard soy sauce. Roll chestnuts in granulated sugar and wrap each chestnut with a small strip of bacon and secure with a toothpick. Arrange on a broiler rack and bake at 375 degrees for 25 minutes. Drain on paper towels and serve.

Cinnamon Crisps
Cut flour tortillas into strips or wedges. Deep-fry in hot oil until golden and puffy. Drain on paper towels and sprinkle with powdered or cinnamon sugar. Serve warm.

Barbeque Bites
Pour a bottle of your favorite barbeque sauce over meatballs, cut up frankfurters, or tiny pre-cooked sausages. Heat slowly in a crock pot or in a saucepan over low heat.

French Bread Pizza
Cut a loaf of French bread in half horizontally and place on a cookie sheet. Spread pizza sauce over each half of the French bread. Top with pepperoni, olives, mushrooms, or any other pizza toppings. Sprinkle with grated mozzarella cheese. Bake at 350 degrees until cheese is melted and the pizzas are warm throughout. Slice pizza into 2" sections to serve.

Layered Taco Dip
Spread a large platter with refried beans. Mix together 1 carton of sour cream, 1/2 cup mayonnaise, and 1 package of taco seasoning mix. Spread mixture over the bean layer. Mash 2-3 avocados and mix with the juice of 1 lemon. Spread over sour cream mixture. Continue to layer dip with chopped onions, chopped tomatoes, and chopped olives. Sprinkle top with grated cheddar cheese. Serve with tortilla chips.

FOOTBALL FEVER!

New Year's Day is often spent watching football games. The following are some great snack ideas for football fans to munch on. May the best team win!

FOOTBALL SANDWICHES

- *Score some points with these football-shaped sandwiches.*

Pumpernickel, dark rye,
       or any variety bread slices
Cold cut meat slices
Cheese slices
Tomato slices
Pickle slices
Lettuce
Mustard
Mayonnaise
Cream cheese

Using a football-shaped cookie cutter (purchase a round metal cookie cutter and bend to make a football shape or bend a clean empty vegetable can to use as a cutter), cut bread, cheese, and meat slices. Assemble as you would a sandwich adding lettuce, pickle, tomato, mustard, mayonnaise and other toppings of your choice. To add decorative "football laces," place softened cream cheese in a pastry bag with a round tip. Pipe a line of cream cheese length-wise onto the top of the bread, and add several short lines across the long line to resemble "laces."

CHEESY CHIPS

- *A quick and easy way to dress up potato chips.*

1/2 pkg. crinkle potato chips
1/2 c. grated cheddar cheese
Thyme or marjoram seasoning

Place potato chips on a cookie sheet. Sprinkle grated cheese over the chips. Season lightly with thyme or marjoram. Bake at 350 degrees for 3-5 minutes or until cheese melts. Serve hot.

PIGSKIN POTATOES

- *Baking potatoes are sliced and filled with cheese and bacon.*

Wash and slice baking potatoes into thin slices but not all the way through. (Peel potatoes if desired before slicing.) Place sliced potatoes in a baking dish and sprinkle with melted butter and parmesan cheese. Bake at 350 degrees until potatoes are tender but still slightly crisp. Remove from oven and sprinkle potatoes with grated cheese and crumbled bacon making sure to press some into each slit. Return to oven and bake until potatoes are tender and cheese is melted. Sprinkle with chopped chives. Potatoes can be baked in a microwave if desired. Serve hot.

FOOTBALL BREAD BOWL

- *A creative way to serve vegetable dip to all your football fans.*

Make your favorite homemade bread dough or purchase frozen dough. Varieties of bread such as rye, sourdough, pumpernickel, white, or wheat work well. Shape dough into a large oval which resembles a football. (Make smaller for individual serving sizes.) Place on a lightly greased cookie sheet. Let rise and bake as directed. Bread should be golden brown in color. When done, remove from oven and brush with margarine. Let cool. Cut an oval piece from the top of the bread and remove soft interior leaving approximately 3/4" thick walls. Fill "bowl" with dips, chili, soup, etc. Ask your local bakery to bake a football loaf for you if you would like to purchase one ready-made.

TOUCHDOWN TACO SOUP

- *A hearty meal. So quick and easy it can be made during half-time!*

> 1 lb. ground beef
> 1 large onion, chopped
> 1 can (16 oz.) kidney beans, drained
> 1 can (16 oz.) whole kernel corn, drained
> 1 can (28 oz.) stewed tomatoes
> 1 can (8 oz.) tomato sauce
> 1 pkg. dry taco seasoning mix

Brown ground beef with onion and drain. Place in a large cooking pot and add remaining ingredients. Stir well. Let soup simmer for about 30 minutes to blend flavors. Sprinkle with grated cheese and crushed tortilla shells to serve. Garnish with a dollop of sour cream.

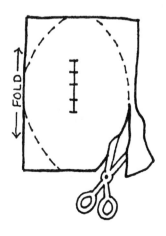

FOOTBALL NAPKINS

- *Turn brown paper napkins into football-shaped napkins.*

Purchase brown or tan colored paper dinner or beverage napkins from a party supply store. Cut each napkin into a football shape making sure to leave part of the folded edge intact. Football laces can be drawn on with a white permanent marker.

BANANA BOATS

- *Yummy filled bananas for a half-time treat.*

      6 large bananas, peeled
      1 container (12 oz.) whipped topping
      4 red apples, chopped
      4 large Snickers brand candy bars, chopped
      1/2 c. nuts, chopped
      Maraschino cherries

Wash bananas and slit length-wise leaving 1" uncut from each end. Cut away about 1/2" of peel on either side of the slit. Scoop out the banana fruit and mash with a fork. Mix with whipped topping, chopped apples, and chopped candy bars. Amount of apples and candy bars can be increased or decreased according to individual tastes. Spoon mixture back into banana peel shells, sprinkle with nuts, and top with a maraschino cherry. A plastic football pick adds a finishing touch for the big game. Serve immediately to prevent bananas from browning. Serves six.

FOOTBALL PIZZA

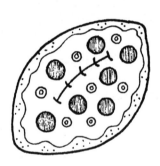

- *Pizza lovers and football fans will love this!*

Make your favorite pizza dough. Shape dough into a football shape. Spread dough with pizza sauce and top with pizza toppings. Sprinkle with grated cheese. Bake according to dough recipe until cheese melts and crust is done. Place some pizza sauce in a heavy-duty plastic bag and snip the corner. Squeeze the sauce onto the pizza over the cheese to resemble laces on a football.

TACO POPCORN

- *A fun popcorn with a Mexican flair.*

      3 Tbs. butter or margarine
      1 1/2 tsp. dry taco mix
      1 1/2 tsp. chopped chives
      2 qts. popped popcorn

Melt butter and stir in taco mix and chives. Pour mixture over the popped popcorn and mix together.

HALF-TIME POPCORN BAR

- *Let each person create their own flavor of popcorn.*

Place a large bowl of popped popcorn in the center of a table along with separate bowls of melted butter, parmesan cheese, taco seasoning, garlic salt, grated cheese, grated chocolate, chives, etc. There are numerous items that can be used for popcorn toppings. Be creative! Give everyone several small bowls and let them garnish their popcorn as desired.

VALENTINE'S DAY

COOKIE LOLLIPOPS

- *A delicious chocolate lollipop made from creme filled cookies.*

    1 pkg. Double Stuf creme filled sandwich cookies
        (Oreo brand cookies with twice the filling)
    1 lb. dipping chocolate or semi-sweet summer coating
    Lollipop sticks
    Seasonal candies, candy sprinkles, chopped nuts, coconut, etc.

Melt chocolate over low heat in a double boiler. Carefully open cookies and cut a notch out of the creme filling for the lollipop sticks to fit into. Dip end of lollipop sticks into chocolate and insert a stick into each notch. Put the cookies back together. (A tiny bit of chocolate may be needed on the creme filling to help cookies stick back together well.) Let set until chocolate is firm.

Holding the lollipop stick, gently dip cookie into the melted chocolate. Use a knife to help spread the chocolate over the entire cookie. Immediately dip lollipop partially in candy sprinkles, nuts, or coconut. Seasonal candies also look cute placed on the center of each lollipop. (Try conversation hearts, frosted animal cookies, M&M brand candies, small molded chocolates, etc.) Lay onto waxed paper to set.

Place lollipops into small plastic lollipop bags or wrap with plastic wrap. Tie with ribbons, jute, or raffia. Decorate for any holiday. Makes a great gift!

BASKET OF KISSES

- *Chocolate candy kisses cover the outside of this "sweet" basket.*

Purchase a large bag of red and pink-foil-wrapped chocolate kisses and a small flat woven basket or other container. Using tacky or hot glue, attach the base of each kiss to the outside of the basket or container. Place kisses side by side and cover entire outside of basket except the bottom. Fill with Valentine treats and give to that special someone!

CHOCOLATE BOWLS

- *Individual dessert cups made by using inflated balloons.*

 Melt semi-sweet dipping chocolate in the microwave or in a double boiler. Pour onto a small plate so chocolate is approximately 1/2" thick. Blow up a small balloon. (Any size balloon will work but small water balloon size work great for individual servings.) Roll the bottom of balloon gently in chocolate rocking back and forth to coat lower 1/3 of balloon. Place on a flat plate covered with waxed or parchment paper. Place in freezer for several minutes or until chocolate is set. Roll in chocolate again to give a second coat and return to freezer. When chocolate is set, pop balloon and gently peel from chocolate. This will create a small, smooth chocolate bowl. Fill with any type of fruit, ice cream, pudding, chocolate mousse, or the following Cherry Pie Salad or Raspberry Dream.

RASPBERRY DREAM

- *Serve as a creamy salad or dessert.*

    1 large pkg. (4.6 oz.) vanilla pudding
        mix, (cooked type)
    1 large pkg. (6 oz.) raspberry gelatin
    2 c. water
    1 tsp. lemon juice
    1 container (16 oz.) whipped topping
    2 c. fresh raspberries

Combine pudding, gelatin, water, and lemon juice in a sauce pan and stir over medium heat until mixture comes to a boil. Remove from heat and pour into a bowl and refrigerate until mixture has thickened. Beat the thick mixture until creamy. Fold in whipped topping and fresh raspberries. Serve in the Chocolate Bowls above if desired.

CHERRY PIE SALAD

- *A wonderful treat!*

    1 can (30 oz.) cherry pie filling
    1 can (8 oz.) crushed pineapple
    1 can (14 oz.) sweetened condensed
        milk
    1 container (8 oz.) whipped topping

Combine all ingredients and chill. Serve in Chocolate Bowls above for a dessert or salad.

ICE CREAM HEART-WICHES

- *An ice cream sandwich you will love!*

Make your favorite sugar cookie dough. Tint the dough pink with food coloring. Roll dough out to 1/4" thickness and using a 4" - 5" heart-shaped cookie cutter, cut dough into hearts and bake as directed. Let cool. Slice vanilla ice cream into 3/4" slices. Cut sliced ice cream with the heart-shaped cookie cutter and immediately place ice cream between two heart cookies making a sandwich. Roll the sides where ice cream is exposed into red and pink candy sprinkles or chopped nuts. Wrap with plastic wrap and freeze. Can be made several days before serving.

12

SOFT SUGAR COOKIES

- *A perfect recipe for cut-out cookies.*

    1 1/2 c. butter or margarine
    1 1/2 c. granulated sugar
    2 eggs
    1 Tbs. vanilla
    2 Tbs. milk
    2 Tbs. baking powder
    1/2 tsp. salt
    4 c. flour

Cream together butter and sugar. Add eggs, vanilla, and milk. Sift together dry ingredients and add to creamed mixture to form a soft dough. Roll out dough to 1/2" thickness and cut into shapes with cookie cutters. Bake at 350 degrees for 8-10 minutes. Decorate as desired or use one of the fun ideas below.

1. **Create a picture perfect cookie.** Cut small motifs from wrapping paper, Valentine cards, or use a color copy of a photograph. Place on top of iced cookies and gently press in the icing to adhere. Remove before eating.

2. **Color and flavor the cookie dough.** Knead food coloring and extract into sugar cookie dough then bake. A nice holiday combination is red coloring with strawberry flavoring. Other nice combinations include green-lime, yellow-lemon, and orange-orange. Add some cocoa for a nice chocolate flavor. Dry gelatin powder can also be used to add flavor and color to the dough.

3. **Paint cookies with egg yolk paint.** Add red (or any color) food coloring to beaten egg yolks. Add several teaspoons of water to thin mixture if needed. Paint on unbaked cookies with a new paintbrush. (Make sure each color dries before painting a different color on the cookie.) Bake as directed. Cookies will come out with bright, shiny colors.

4. **Knead candy sprinkles into the cookie dough.** Press sprinkles into the tops of cookies before baking. No need to frost.

5. **Make a giant heart cookie.** Cut a large paper heart to be used for a pattern. Lay the paper pattern on rolled-out dough and cut around pattern with a table knife. Carefully transfer the cut-out heart cookie to a cookie sheet and bake. Decorate and write a Valentine message on the giant cookie.

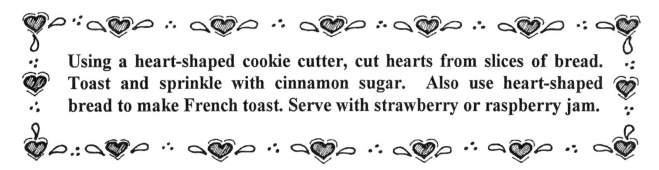

Using a heart-shaped cookie cutter, cut hearts from slices of bread. Toast and sprinkle with cinnamon sugar. Also use heart-shaped bread to make French toast. Serve with strawberry or raspberry jam.

CHERRY CHOCOLATE ECLAIRS

- *Easy and elegant.*

Pastry
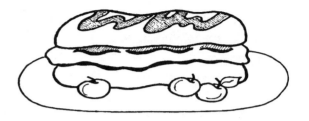

    1/2 c. butter or margarine
    1 c. water
    1/4 tsp. salt
    1 c. flour
    4 eggs

In a saucepan, bring water and butter to a boil. Remove from heat and add salt and flour. With a wooden spoon, stir vigorously until mixture forms a ball and leaves the side of the pan. Cool slightly. Add eggs one at a time to flour mixture, beating well after each one. Beat mixture until smooth. (To make a chocolate pastry, add 2 tablespoons of cocoa and 1 tablespoon granulated sugar to pastry before adding eggs. After filling, sprinkle tops with powdered sugar instead of icing.)

Using a tablespoon or a pastry tube without the tip, make mounds of dough 4" x 1 1/2" on a greased cookie sheet. Bake at 400 degrees for 35-40 minutes until the pastry shells are golden brown. Make a slit in the side of each shell and bake for 5 minutes more. Remove from oven and allow to cool.

Filling
    1 small pkg. (3.4 oz.) vanilla instant pudding mix
    1 1/2 c. milk
    1/2 c. plain yogurt
    Cherry pie filling

Combine first three ingredients and mix well. Allow to chill until set. Split pastry shells and remove any soft dough inside. Fill shells with a layer of the cream filling mixture. Spoon cherry pie filling over the cream filling, replace the pastry tops, and frost with chocolate icing (below). (Pastry shells can be filled with any cream or fruit filling. For a nice meal, fill with hot or cold chicken salad.)

Chocolate Icing
    2 squares semi-sweet chocolate
    2 Tbs. butter or margarine
    1 c. powdered sugar
    3 Tbs. milk or water

Melt chocolate and butter in a saucepan over low heat. Stir in powdered sugar and milk until smooth. Spread icing on the top of each eclair. If thicker icing is desired, add more powdered sugar or cocoa.

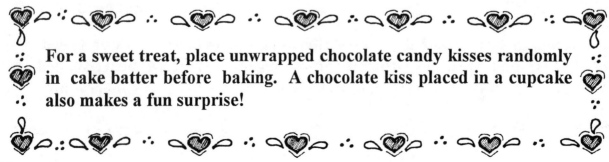

For a sweet treat, place unwrapped chocolate candy kisses randomly in cake batter before baking. A chocolate kiss placed in a cupcake also makes a fun surprise!

ROCKY ROAD HEARTS

- *Your heart will skip a beat for this treat.*

  1 lb. milk or semi-sweet chocolate chips
  1 c. chopped nuts
  1/2 c. raisins or cut-up dried fruit
  1 c. miniature marshmallows
  1 c. mini M&M brand candies

Melt chocolate chips in a double boiler. Lightly grease 3" heart-shaped cookie cutters and place on a greased cookie sheet. Pour 1/2" of chocolate into each cookie cutter. Immediately sprinkle nuts, raisins, marshmallows, and candies on the chocolate to form another layer. Drizzle remaining chocolate over the toppings. Allow chocolate to set well before removing from cookie cutters. *Note:* For a peanut butter flavor, stir 1/4 cup peanut butter into the melted chocolate.

PEANUT BUTTER CUPS

- *These peanut butter cups will impress your favorite Valentine!*

  1 c. margarine
  6 c. powdered sugar
  2 c. creamy peanut butter
  Dash salt
  Dipping chocolate
  Mini paper candy cups

Mix together margarine, powdered sugar, peanut butter, and salt. (Adjust amounts of powdered sugar to make a soft, pliable dough.) Roll dough into small, marble-sized balls. Melt chocolate in a double boiler over low heat. Place a small amount of chocolate into each paper candy cup coating the bottom and the sides. Slightly flatten peanut butter ball and place in the paper cup on top of the chocolate. Cover the peanut butter ball with more melted chocolate. Refrigerate to set.

SWEETHEART TARTS

- *Delicious tarts with a cream cheese pastry.*

  1 c. butter
  1 pkg. (8 oz.) cream cheese
  2 c. flour
  1 can (20 oz.) fruit pie filling
        (cherry, apple, blueberry, etc.)

Soften butter and cream cheese. Combine and mix well. Add flour and mix into a ball. Roll dough out like a pie crust about 1/8" thick. Press pieces of rolled out pastry into small tart pans. Place tart pans on a cookie sheet and bake at 375 degrees for 15-20 minutes or until light brown. Let cool and remove tart shells from pans. Fill shells with fruit filling and top with a dollop of whipped topping to serve.

To make **turnovers**, roll pastry 1/8" thick. Cut 5" circles. Place several tablespoons of fruit filling on each circle and fold over. Crimp edges with a fork. Place turnovers on an ungreased cookie sheet and bake at 375 degrees for 15-20 minutes or until light brown. Let cool slightly and drizzle with a thin, powdered sugar icing or serve warm with ice cream. Makes approximately 15 tarts.

CHOCOLATE CHEWS

- *Mold this chocolate candy into a kiss!*

  2 squares unsweetened chocolate
  2 Tbs. butter or margarine
  1/2 c. light corn syrup
  1 tsp. vanilla
  3/4 c. powdered milk
  3 c. powdered sugar

Melt together butter, chocolate, and corn syrup. Blend well. Add vanilla, powdered milk, and powdered sugar. Knead until a soft dough forms. Roll into logs and wrap with waxed paper or mold into a chocolate kiss and wrap in foil. Add a paper message at the top of the kiss.

15

CUPID CRISPS

- *This macaroon type cookie will capture your heart.*

Remove crusts from slices of white sandwich bread. Cut each slice of bread into 3 strips or cut bread into heart shapes using a cookie cutter. Dip bread pieces into sweetened condensed milk and then roll into flaked coconut. Place coated bread pieces on a well greased cookie sheet and bake at 375 degrees for 8-10 minutes. When done, immediately remove from cookie sheet.

APPLE LIPS

- *Create a "sweet teeth" snack.*

Cut 2 red apple wedges 1/2" wide. Place peanut butter or cream cheese on one side of each. Place together with red apple skin side facing front. Place miniature marshmallows or small, white candy hearts between layers to look like "teeth." Kids love this snack!

COOKIE CUTTERS FULL OF LOVE

- *Heart-shaped cookie cutters filled with a sweet treat.*

Melt vanilla flavored almond bark in a microwave or in a double boiler. Gently stir in crushed, red peppermint candies. (Determine amounts by taste and the number of cookie cutters being filled.) Place a small metal heart-shaped cookie cutter on a cookie sheet lined with foil. Pour almond bark mixture into the cookie cutter filling it almost to the top. Place in refrigerator until mixture is firm. Do not remove the cookie cutter from the almond bark mixture. Wrap the heart in cellophane or plastic wrap and add a card that states, "You are a *sweet*-heart" or "A *sweet*-heart for you!"

RASPBERRY SHORTBREAD HEARTS

- *Melt-in-your-mouth cookies.*

    2 c. flour
    6 Tbs. granulated sugar
    2 Tbs. cornstarch
    1 c. butter or margarine

Combine flour, sugar, and cornstarch. Mix well. Cut in butter until crumbly. Form into a ball and chill for one hour. Roll out dough to 1/4" thickness. Using a 3" or 4" heart-shaped cookie cutter, cut heart shapes from dough. Top with raspberry topping (below) and bake at 375 degrees for 8 minutes. Cool and drizzle with melted semi-sweet chocolate chips.

Raspberry Topping
Place 1/2 cup red raspberry jam (seedless) and 2 1/2 teaspoons cornstarch in a saucepan. Heat to boiling stirring constantly. Remove from heat and let cool. (Any type of jam or preserves will work. Blackberry or strawberry jam also make nice Valentine cookies.)

SWEET-TALK POPCORN TREATS

- *Conversation heart popcorn ball for your sweetheart.*

    6 c. miniature marshmallows
    1/4 c. butter or margarine
    4 qts. popped popcorn
    1 c. red and pink M&M brand candies
    1 c. roasted peanuts
    1 c. candy conversation hearts

Melt marshmallows and margarine in a heavy saucepan over medium heat, stirring constantly. In a large bowl, combine popped corn, M&M candies, peanuts, and conversation hearts. Pour marshmallow mixture over ingredients in the bowl and toss to coat evenly. Pour into a greased 9" x 13" pan and let cool. Cut into squares to serve. Mixture can also be made into popcorn balls. Add a wooden stick and wrap with cellophane to give as a gift. Tie with a pretty bow.

HEART PIZZA

- *Heart-shaped pepperoni makes this pizza extra special.*

To make a pizza "covered with love," either buy a pizza without pepperoni or make a homemade pizza. Purchase thinly sliced pepperoni, mozzarella cheese, and a small heart-shaped cookie cutter approximately 1" in diameter. Cut pepperoni and thinly sliced mozzarella cheese into heart shapes. Arrange pepperoni and cheese hearts on pizza. Bake as directed.

CANDY KISS ROSE

- *A rose that is extra sweet.*

    2 red or pink-foil-wrapped chocolate candy kisses
    12" piece of floral stem wire
    5" x 7" piece of clear cellophane
    Green silk rose leaves
    Green florist tape

Gently insert one end of the wire into the pointed end of one of the foil-wrapped chocolate kisses. Place the base of the other chocolate kiss against the base of the first as illustrated. Center cellophane over kisses and pull down to cover the kisses. Gently twist cellophane around wire and wrap with florist tape to secure. Wrap entire wire with the florist tape adding a rose leaf several inches down from the kisses. Make several candy kiss roses and place in a rose box from a florist or fill a vase full. A clever gift!

DECORATE WITH CHOCOLATE

- *Garnish Valentine desserts with chocolate!*

Chocolate Leaves
Brush the back of non-toxic leaves with melted chocolate. Let set in refrigerator or freezer. Gently peel off leaves and use the chocolate leaves to garnish cakes and other desserts.

Chocolate Curls
Gently slide a vegetable peeler over a large candy bar or a large block of white or dark chocolate at room temperature. Chocolate curls will form. For a unique decorating idea using chocolate curls, pile on top of a chocolate heart cake, white curls on one half of the cake and dark curls on the other half.

Chocolate Fancies
Fill a pastry bag with melted chocolate and using a small round tip, squeeze chocolate designs onto waxed paper. (A heavy duty plastic bag with the corner snipped off will work well in place of a pastry bag.) Squeeze chocolate onto a simple outline placed under the waxed paper or make random designs with the chocolate. Try hearts, initials, squiggly lines, etc. Let set and use to garnish ice cream, cream pies, or other desserts.

Chocolate Crinkle Cups
Brush the inside of a paper cupcake liner with melted chocolate. Let chocolate set until firm. Remove paper liner. Use chocolate crinkle cups to serve ice cream or soft desserts in.

Chocolate Roses
Melt 10 ounces of semi-sweet chocolate chips or chocolate flavored almond bark in a double boiler over low heat or in the microwave. Add to the melted chocolate 1/3 cup light corn syrup. Stir well and pour approximately 1/2" of chocolate mixture onto a sheet of waxed paper. Cover with waxed paper and leave for several hours until mixture is pliable. Chocolate will become like a soft clay and can be molded into any shape.

To form an edible chocolate rose, roll several small chocolate balls and flatten to make round disks. Roll one disk into a cone shape. Wrap two other disks around the cone to make a rosebud. Each chocolate disk will form a petal as it is wrapped on the rosebud. Continue to wrap chocolate disks around the rosebud until desired size rose is reached. Use chocolate roses to decorate cakes or place on wooden skewers or small dowels to make a bouquet. Roses will harden after several days. Store chocolate roses in a cool, dry place.

CUPID CANDY BARS

- *A delicious way to say "I love you!"*

Purchase candy bars that are covered with chocolate. Any shaped candy bar will work well. Unwrap candy bar and using Royal Icing (see page 102), write a message on the candy bar using a pastry bag with a small round tip. Add a few rose buds and leaves on one end or attach a candy heart with icing. Decorate for any holiday or use for an invitation, a thank you, a favor, etc.

GIFT TRAY GOODIES

- *A unique container for Valentine treats.*

Purchase a divided plastic silverware tray. Fill each section of the tray with different kinds of cookies or Valentine candies. Small Valentine related gifts can also be placed in the tray. Wrap tray in cellophane for a nice gift. Tie with curling ribbon and attach a Valentine card.

SCOOP OF LOVE

- *A scoop of candy kisses for your Valentine.*

Fill a plastic measuring scoop with red and pink-foil-wrapped candy kisses or other Valentine candy. Wrap with cellophane and tie on a pretty ribbon. Attach a tag that states "A scoop of my love for you!"

"SOUPER" VALENTINE

- *Great idea for a co-worker.*

Cover the label of a soup can with a piece of pink or red wrapping paper. Place a bow on top and a Valentine tag that states "You are a *souper* friend," or "To my *souper* sweetheart."

CREPE PURSES

- *A chocolate or fruit surprise inside!*

Make crepes using your favorite crepe recipe and let cool. Place a candy kiss, chocolate truffle, or whole strawberry in the center of each crepe. Wrap crepe around each item and gather like a package. Tie with a pretty ribbon and use at each place setting at a holiday dinner or as a party favor. (These purses can also be made using phyllo dough.)

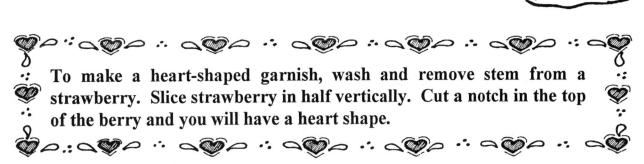

To make a heart-shaped garnish, wash and remove stem from a strawberry. Slice strawberry in half vertically. Cut a notch in the top of the berry and you will have a heart shape.

A VALENTINE TABLE

- *Decorate a table even cupid would love.*

Elegant Chairs
For a beautiful and unique way to seat your guests, decorate each dining room chair. Using wide strips of tulle (net), tie a bow with several loops. Do the same using wide satin ribbon. Leave several long streamers hanging down from each bow. Place the two bows together and with a small ribbon secure to the back of each chair. Attach a place card in the center of each bow so guests will know where they are to be seated.

Valentine Card Placemats
Have children recycle Valentine cards received from school by making placemats. In addition to Valentine cards, use glitter, paper doilies, stickers, markers, etc. and decorate a piece of lightweight cardstock the size of a placemat. When finished decorating the cardstock, cover with clear contact paper or take to a copy center and laminate for durability. (A great way to recycle Christmas cards.)

Lacy Heart Tablecloth
Lay various sizes of paper heart doilies on a paper or fabric tablecloth. Use spray adhesive on doilies to help hold in place. Using red spray paint, gently spray over the doilies and remove to reveal lacy hearts.

Candy Heart Napkin Rings
To make a fun Valentine napkin ring, cut a piece of pink or red cardstock 1" x 7". Glue ends together to form a ring. Glue candy conversation hearts around the entire cardstock ring in a single row or glue one large foil-wrapped chocolate heart on the ring. Place a napkin through the ring to use.

Waffle Cone Favors
Fill a purchased waffle ice cream cone with Valentine candies and wrap with cellophane. Children love this treat and they can eat the container too! A great idea for room mothers.

Muffin Tin Candle Holder
Want a quick candle holder for that romantic evening? Place red and white votive candles in the cups of a muffin tin. Hearts can be stencilled around the rim of the pan with acrylic paint. The muffin tin can also be antiqued (purchase antique medium at a craft store) for a country look. Cute and easy!

NEIGHBORHOOD VALENTINES

- *Let red, white, and pink helium balloons be an invitation to a party.*

Share some Valentine spirit throughout your neighborhood! Purchase a bouquet of red, white, and pink helium balloons with a ribbon attached to each balloon. Place a balloon on the front lawn of each of your neighbors. Secure balloon by tying the ribbon to a nail or a florist pin and pressing it into the ground. Attach a card that states, "Happy Valentine's Day!" Balloons can also be a creative way to invite friends to a party at your home; just attach an invitation to the ribbon. You may also wish to cover an entire yard with helium balloons to surprise someone special.

SACK OF LOVE NOTES

- *Make a collection of fun Valentines for your sweetheart. A great idea and economical too!*

By using small items commonly found around your home, you can create notes of love to give to someone special. Tuck the notes in places they will be sure to be found, or fill a small cellophane bag and give at a romantic candlelight dinner.

Cut 2" x 4" cards from lightweight cardstock. Decorative paper scissors can be used for a lacy look. Write a different message on each card and then glue or attach the small item that corresponds to each message onto the card. Here are some ideas to help get you started. The possibilities are endless so be creative!

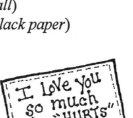

You **light** my fire! (*match stick*)
You **stretch** my imagination! (*rubber band*)
My heart **bursts** for you! (*balloon*)
You were **mint** to be mine! (*a small mint candy*)
I'm glad I **picked** you to be mine! (*toothpick*)
Just the thought of you makes me **pop**! (*popcorn kernels*)
I **chews** you to be mine! (*stick of gum*)
My nights with you are a **ball**! (*small star stickers and a small rubber ball*)
You are **music** to my ears! (*small music note stickers or note cut from black paper*)
You **charge** my battery! (*small battery*)
I'm **soft** on you! (*cotton ball*)
You are **hot**! (*small packet of hot sauce*)

You are a **Q**- tee! (*cotton swab*)
You have my **stamp** of approval! (*cancelled postage stamp*)
You **drive** me crazy! (*small toy car*)
You make **cents** to me! (*penny or chocolate coin*)
I love you so much it **hurts**! (*adhesive bandage*)
You make me **melt**! (*wrapped chocolate*)
You are my **honey**! (*small packet of honey*)
I love you so much its **scary**! (*Halloween sticker or a small plastic spider*)
You have all the **bear** necessities! (*cinnamon bear*)
I was a **smartie** when I chose you! (*Smarties brand candy*)
You captured my **heart**! (*small bag of heart candies or a heart chocolate*)
My heart **beets** for you! (*small can of beets*)
You have the **key** to my heart! (*key*)

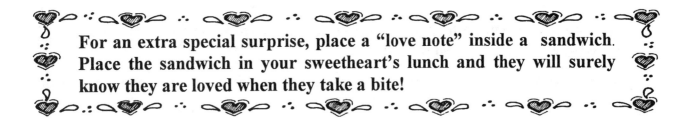

For an extra special surprise, place a "love note" inside a sandwich. Place the sandwich in your sweetheart's lunch and they will surely know they are loved when they take a bite!

SEND A VALENTINE

- *Here are some clever Valentines for your friends and family.*

Anonymous Valentines
Start a fun tradition by sending an anonymous Valentine to someone. Choose several different people each year or send a card to the same person year after year. Send a card to someone who may not receive many Valentines.

Family Card Box
Make a family Valentine box or sack. This would be a great project for kids to work on. Ask family members to make Valentine cards for each other during the week and place in the box or sack. Open the family Valentine box Valentine's night and enjoy the contents as a family.

Fourteen Days of Valentines
Try this fun idea for a friend, neighbor, or for your sweetheart! Give one small Valentine gift secretly each day. Start on February 1st and continue through the 14th. The gifts can remain anonymous or the giver can be revealed on Valentine's Day.

Photo Valentine
To send a greeting of love to someone far away, cut out a large heart from pink or red construction paper and write a simple greeting with bold letters on the heart. Hold up the heart with the message, or place on a babies lap, and have someone take a photograph. Balloons can be included in the photo for a special effect. Great for grandparents!

Smooooooch Card
Pucker up to make a crazy Valentine card for that special guy by using lipstick and real kisses. Have each girl put on a bright color of lipstick and kiss a pre-made card leaving a kiss imprint. Each girl will then sign under her kiss. The more kisses and signatures on the card the better! This is especially fun for teenagers and young single adults. Remember, an old tube of lipstick can also be a great tool for leaving a message on a mirror, a car window, or a window in your home.

Secret Letters
Using a white crayon, write a Valentine message on plain white paper. On a separate sheet of paper write instructions on how to reveal the message. Messages can be revealed by brushing watercolor paints over the paper.

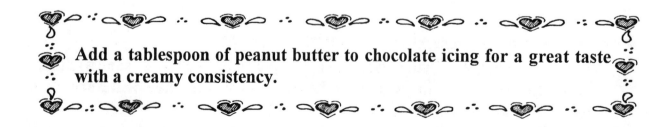

Add a tablespoon of peanut butter to chocolate icing for a great taste with a creamy consistency.

CANDY BAR TREASURE HUNT

- *Sweet clues lead to a Valentine treasure.*

Create a candy bar treasure hunt for your sweetheart! Hide candy bars with clues so they lead to the candy bar and clue. Have a special treasure at the end of the hunt (candlelight dinner, movie tickets, etc.). Below are some ideas to help you get started. Candy bar brand names are in bold type.

U-NO I love you!   *Look under the kitchen table.*
Here's a **HUG(S)** for you!   *Look in the mailbox.*
Your love sends me to the **MILKY WAY**!   *Look behind the television.*
I get **BUTTERFINGERS** around you!   *Look in the refrigerator.*
I was a **SMARTIE(S)** when I married you!   *Look under your pillow.*
Everyday is a **PAYDAY** when I am with you!   *Look in your coat pocket.*
My love for you is worth more than **$100,000**!   *Look by the back door.*
Your **KISSES** send me to **MARS**!   *Look in the car.*
You are my **LIFESAVER**!   *Look in your slippers.*
I am **NUTS** (can of nuts) over you!

Candy bars can also be used to create a Valentine message poster. Write a message on a piece of poster board and tape on different candy bars to where words normally would be written. For example, "You are my **BIG HUNK** and I love you more than **U-NO**!" (The **BIG HUNK** and **U-NO** candy bars would be taped to the poster instead of writing the words.) Make the message long enough to cover the poster board and use numerous candy bars.

PHOTO BOUQUET

- *Heart-shaped photos make up part of this bouquet.*

Gather creative or special snapshots of you, your sweetheart, etc. Using a heart template (heart-shaped cookie cutter, cardboard heart, or heart stencil), trace a heart onto the photo. Cut out the heart along the traced line being careful to leave the area of the photo you wish to be seen inside the heart. A 3" to 4" size heart is a nice size to use for this bouquet.

Purchase some green floral stem wire from your florist or local craft store. Tape each photo heart onto a piece of the stem wire with clear tape. Arrange photo heart "flowers" in a vase and add a pretty bow. Be sure to add some fern and babies breath and other live flowers and greenery to complete the arrangement.

A photo bouquet makes a unique gift! It is also a creative centerpiece idea for a baby or wedding shower, a birthday party, or for a family dinner using a photo of each person present. Cut photos into any shape or cut around the subject in photos freehand.

VALENTINE PARTY GAMES

- *Having a party this year? Try some of these fun games.*

Half-a-Heart Game

A Valentine game for singles or teenagers. This makes for good mingling especially with a large group. Cut Valentine cards or paper hearts in half like a puzzle, creating two pieces. Separate pieces into two piles, making sure that the matching pieces are in separate piles. As guests arrive at the party, give them a puzzle piece. Give male guests a card from one pile and female guests a card from the opposite pile. As guests mingle, have them search for the person who has the other half of their card. The two people then become partners for a game or dinner.

Mystery Messages

A game for a married couples party. Give each person a heart-shaped piece of paper and a pencil. Have everyone write a Valentine message to their spouse without mentioning their name. Allow about 10 minutes then collect the hearts and have the host or hostess read them aloud one at a time. As each message is read everyone tries to guess who the message is written to.

Candy Conversation Story

Fill a bowl with Valentine candy conversation hearts. Have party guests sit in a circle. Choose one person to start the game by taking a candy heart from the bowl. That person starts a story of his own creation and must include the words from the candy heart in the story. He then passes the bowl to the next person who chooses a candy heart and continues the story. This continues around the circle with each person adding to the story and using the words from the candy hearts. This game often creates a lot of laughter from the crazy story lines!

Tied Spoons

To play this game, everyone will need a partner. Have the partners sit across from each other at a table. Place a bowl of ice cream in front of each person. Give the partners two spoons that have been tied together with yarn or string so they are about 12" apart. At the word "GO," the partners eat their bowls of ice cream as fast as they can. The first set of partners to finish their ice cream wins.

HOMEMADE STICKERS

- *A great recipe for making personalized stickers.*

In a microwave oven, bring 4 tablespoons of vinegar to a boil. Mix in 2 packages unflavored gelatin and stir until dissolved. Add 1 1/2 teaspoons peppermint extract or extract of your choice. Brush the solution onto the back of paper to be used for stickers. Use plain paper, wrapping paper, magazine pages, etc. Let dry. Cut stickers to desired size and lick to stick. Perforations can be made by using a sewing machine with no thread in the needle. This will make individual squares that resemble postage stamps. If plain paper is used, decorate each "stamp" with rubber stamps, markers, or crayons. Store leftover sticker solution in an airtight container and gently warm when ready to use again as mixture will solidify.

ST. PATRICK'S DAY

GREEN GAME

- *Great party game for a large group.*

Give guests a list of the following statements as they arrive at your St. Patrick's Day party. Each guest must have another guest sign his/her name after a statement that applies to him/her. Each person can only sign once. Set a time limit and enjoy the fun!

SOMEONE WHO…

has green eyes
is wearing green socks
has visited Ireland
has a friend named Patrick
has picked a shamrock
has a neighbor with the name of Green
is wearing a green shirt
has tried to find the end of the rainbow
has cooked a corned beef brisket
has a favorite food that is green

has a green couch
drives a green car
wears green pajamas
has seen the film *Anne of Green Gables*
likes Irish Soda Bread
has a lot of good luck
has a pot of gold at home (jar of coins)
has not read the story *Green Eggs and Ham*
has seen a real leprechaun
has a birthday in March

GRAB FOR GOLD

- *Children reach into a "jar of gold."*

Each night, have Dad and Mom place all their loose pocket change into a large jar. On St. Patrick's Day, let children reach in with one hand and scoop up as many coins as they can hold. The children get to keep all the coins they grasp and pull out of the jar.

LIME COOKIES

- *Make cut-out shamrock cookies from this delicious dough.*

1 1/2 c. margarine
1 c. granulated sugar
1 small pkg. (3 oz.) lime flavored gelatin
1 egg
1 tsp. baking powder
1 tsp. vanilla
4 1/2 c. flour
Green candy sprinkles (opt.)

Cream together margarine, sugar, and gelatin. Add egg, vanilla, and baking powder and mix well. Stir in flour and mix until a soft dough forms. Roll out dough on a lightly floured surface and cut out shamrocks using a cookie cutter. Decorate with green candy sprinkles, if desired. Place on an ungreased cookie sheet and bake at 400 degrees for 13-15 minutes.

SHAMROCK CAKE

- *Heart-shaped pans are used to make a shamrock cake.*

Mix two yellow cake mixes (separately) as directed on package and stir a small package of dry pistachio pudding into each cake mix. Add several drops of green food coloring if needed to create a nice green color. Divide batter and pour into three greased and floured heart-shaped baking pans. Bake as directed and let cool. Place pointed ends of cakes together to form a shamrock. Frost the cake with green-tinted whipped cream or green icing. Sprinkle on green colored sugar (1-2 drops green food color to 1/2 cup granulated sugar) or decorate with green candies. A stem for the shamrock cake can be cut from green paper or made from cake batter baked in a small loaf pan. *Note:* To make a four-leaf-clover cake, bake batter in four heart-shaped pans instead of three pans.

LEPRECHAUN DIVINITY

- *A melt-in-your-mouth treat.*

3 c. granulated sugar
3/4 c. light corn syrup
3/4 c. hot water
1/4 tsp. salt

2 egg whites
1 small pkg. (3 oz.) lime flavored gelatin
1 c. nuts, chopped (opt.)

In a heavy saucepan, place sugar, corn syrup, water, and salt. Stir over medium heat until mixture boils and sugar is dissolved. Place lid on pan for 4-5 minutes to allow steam to wash down sugar crystals from sides of pan. Remove lid and boil to hard ball stage (250 degrees F). In a large bowl, beat egg whites until foamy. Add gelatin and beat until stiff peaks form. Pour hot syrup slowly over egg white mixture, beating constantly with electric mixer at high speed until mixture looses its gloss. Stir in nuts if desired. Drop candy by teaspoonfuls onto waxed paper. *Note:* This recipe is great for other holidays. Any flavor of gelatin can be used.

MINTY MALT

- *This drink will please any leprechaun.*

   3/4 c. milk
   1 banana
   2 c. mint flavored ice cream (green)
   1 Tbs. malt (or to taste)

Place all ingredients in a blender and blend until smooth.

LEPRECHAUN DUST

- *Children wake to a leprechaun trail.*

Tuck foil-wrapped chocolate kisses, or gold chocolate coins under a child's pillow while they are sleeping. Sprinkle a tiny bit of gold glitter by the child's pillow and watch the excitement happen when the child awakens! Sprinkle glitter several places around the house and let the child see if he can find where the leprechaun has been!

BASKET OF GOOD LUCK

- *Give someone the luck-o'-the-Irish.*

Fill a basket with green items and add a tag that wishes a Happy St. Patrick's Day! Line the basket with green tissue paper or a plaid green cloth. Be creative when choosing items to fill the basket. The following are some suggestions to get you started:

green fruit	green soda
green socks	green toothbrush
green jelly	green vegetables
green candy	green book
green dinnerware	potted plant
green mouthwash	green stationery
green spices	green notebook

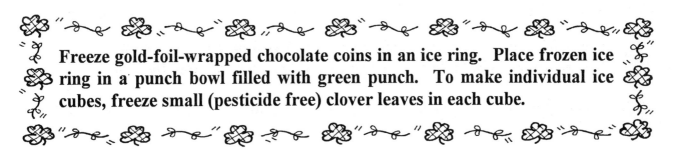

Freeze gold-foil-wrapped chocolate coins in an ice ring. Place frozen ice ring in a punch bowl filled with green punch. To make individual ice cubes, freeze small (pesticide free) clover leaves in each cube.

27

GREEN DINNER PARTY

- *Green, green, everywhere!*

Invite your friends to a "green" dinner party. Request that everyone come dressed in green clothing and bring a green food item to share. Suggested food items may be pickles, lime gelatin, green popcorn, green salad, peas, green beans, pistachio pudding, etc. You will be amazed at the creativity! Make sure to provide a green beverage. A quick and easy table covering can be made for your party by covering the table with white or green butcher paper and painting or stencilling shamrocks onto the paper.

GREEN GUESSES

Shamrock

- *Your thoughts will turn green with this game.*

Give guests a pencil and paper and instruct them to write down as many items as they can think of that are green. Set a time limit and then have guests take turns reading their answers aloud. If two or more people have the same answer, they must cross off the item. The person with the most items that no one else has written down is the winner and receives a green prize.

GREEN TREASURE HUNT

- *Green clues will lead to the hidden treasure.*

Send your children on a treasure hunt through your house and yard. Make clues lead to places or items that are green (lettuce in the refrigerator, couch, tree outside, houseplant, mom's dress in the closet, etc.). For the treasure at the end of the hunt, hide a small black plastic pot full of candy.

HUNT FOR GOLD

- *Let children search for hidden chocolate coins.*

Hide gold-foil-wrapped chocolate coins throughout your house or yard. Give each child a small sack and let them race off to find the coins. A great tradition your children will not forget.

For a fun surprise, wrap a real coin in foil and place in a cupcake before icing. A gold-foil-wrapped chocolate coin can also be used.

EASTER BONNET CAKE

- *A beautiful lemon bonnet with real sugared blossoms.*

Mix one package lemon cake mix according to directions. Stir in 1 teaspoon grated lemon zest. Grease and flour a 1-quart heat safe bowl and a 12" round disposable pizza pan 1/2" deep. Fill bowl 2/3 full with batter and place the remaining batter in pizza pan. Bake at 350 degrees. Bake cake in pizza pan for 15-20 minutes or until a toothpick inserted comes out clean. Bake cake in bowl about 35-40 minutes or until a toothpick inserted in center comes out clean. Cool on wire rack.

 To assemble bonnet cake, place the 12" cake on a large serving plate. Spread a small amount of icing in center. Invert cake from bowl onto center of 12" cake to look like a bonnet. Spread entire cake with Lemon Icing (below).

Decorate bonnet cake with 1 1/2" wide, wire-edged pastel ribbon (1 1/3 yards). Drape ribbon around brim and make a bow as if on a hat. Arrange fresh or sugared flowers at base of crown intertwined in the ribbon. This makes a beautiful centerpiece that can also be served for dessert.

Lemon Icing
>   1 1/2 lbs. powdered sugar
>   1/2 c. margarine
>   4-oz. cream cheese, softened
>   4-5 Tbs. fresh lemon juice
>   3 drops yellow food coloring

Cream together margarine and cream cheese. Beat in powdered sugar and lemon juice. (Add more or less juice to make a spreadable, creamy consistency.) Add yellow food coloring to make a pale yellow color.

To sugar flowers, use non-toxic flower blossoms and leaves, free of pesticides such as rose buds, daisies, pansies, violets, lavender, primroses, mums, or carnations. Beat one egg white until frothy. Using fingers or a pastry brush, gently coat entire blossom with egg white. Sprinkle blossoms with granulated sugar, completely coating them. Tap off excess sugar and lay on waxed paper. Dry 24 hours.

HOMESPUN SUGAR NESTS

- *Serve ice cream or fruit in these elegant spun sugar nests.*

      2 c. granulated sugar
      1/2 c. light corn syrup
      1/4 c. plus 1 Tbs. water
      1 drop oil flavoring
      Pastel paste food coloring

Place all ingredients in a heavy saucepan and cook over medium heat until candy thermometer reaches 310 degrees. Do not stir while mixture is cooking. Remove mixture from heat and allow to set for 2 minutes. When ready to spin the sugar, place two clean 1" dowels across two chairs approximately 1 1/2 feet apart. Place newspaper on the floor under the dowels to catch syrup that will drip. Wrap a rubber band tightly around 2 or more forks, with tines facing outward. Dip fork tines into the hot syrup and allow syrup to drip back into pan until threads begin to form. Quickly move arm back and forth above the two dowels making long threads of sugary candy.

Continue to make threads from syrup. As spun syrup gets several inches thick, remove it from the dowels. Carefully shape spun sugar threads into a circle and depress the center to make a "nest." Serve ice cream, candies, or fruit in the spun sugar nests. Makes 5 nests.

Note: Don't try to make this on a rainy day because humidity will cause candy to be very sticky. Store spun sugar in a cool dry place. Make within several hours of serving.

MARSHMALLOWS

- *A soft, creamy confection.*

      2 c. granulated sugar
      3 envelopes unflavored gelatin
      1/8 tsp. salt
      1 c. water
      1 tsp. vanilla
      Powdered sugar

In saucepan, combine gelatin, sugar, salt, and water. Stir well. Bring to a boil and remove from heat. Cool slightly, and add vanilla. Pour into a large mixer bowl and beat at high speed for 10-15 minutes or until mixture resembles thick marshmallow creme. Pour into a buttered 13" x 9" x 2" pan. Let cool. Cover and let set for several hours or overnight. Cut into 1" squares or cut shapes using cookie cutters. Roll each square or shape in powdered sugar to coat sides. Flavored powdered sugars such as lemon and strawberry make delicious marshmallows!

Chocolate Marshmallow Eggs

Fill a cake pan at least 2" deep with flour. Press a real or plastic egg into the flour making impressions approximately 1" apart. Spoon the marshmallow creme (recipe above) into the impressions. Let set for one hour. Carefully remove the marshmallow eggs from the flour and place on a waxed paper lined plate. Freeze for 30 minutes. Melt dipping chocolate or semi-sweet chocolate chips in a double boiler over low heat. (Add a tiny amount of shortening to the chocolate chips if needed to thin.) Using a spoon, dip the frozen marshmallow eggs in the chocolate to coat. Place on waxed paper to set. Decorate eggs with icing flowers if desired.

POLKA DOT CAKE

- *Accent your cake batter with a rainbow of colors.*

Prepare a white cake mix as directed. Divide batter into 5 bowls. Tint 4 of the bowls of batter different colors using food coloring. Mix well. (Use cocoa powder to make a brown color if desired.) Do not tint the remaining bowl of batter. Spoon batter from each bowl by large spoonfuls into a greased and floured cake pan. Bake as directed. This will create a colorful "polka dotted" cake!

EASTER EGG BREAD

- *Dyed eggs are baked in this flavorful sweet dough ring.*

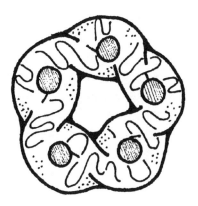

1/4 c. milk
1 envelope active dry yeast
1/3 c. granulated sugar
2 eggs
1/4 c. margarine or butter
1/4 tsp. anise seed, crushed
1/4 tsp. cinnamon
Grated orange or lemon zest

1 tsp. salt
2 1/2-3 c. flour
1/4 c. golden raisins
1/4 c. slivered almonds
5 dyed eggs (raw)
1 beaten egg white
Candy sprinkles (opt.)

Heat milk until warm (120-130 degrees). Sprinkle yeast and 1 teaspoon of sugar into milk. Stir to dissolve. Let set for several minutes until mixture becomes bubbly. In a separate pan, melt margarine and let cool slightly. Beat the two eggs and add to margarine. Add remaining sugar, cinnamon, salt, orange zest, and anise seed. Mix together well. Add yeast and milk mixture.

Add flour 1/2 cup at a time to the mixture. Add enough flour until mixture forms a soft dough and is not sticky. Knead for 6 minutes or until smooth and elastic. Place dough in a greased bowl and cover. Let rise in a warm place until doubled.

Punch dough down and knead in almonds and raisins. Roll into two ropes, each 24" long. Place on a lightly greased cookie sheet. Twist ropes together and form into a ring. Make at least 5 twists. Pinch ends together. Place a dyed, raw egg between each twist of the dough. Eggs will be hard-cooked after baking.

Brush dough with beaten egg white and sprinkle on colored candies if desired. Let rise until doubled. Bake in a 350 degree oven for 25-30 minutes. If necessary, cover with foil the last 10 minutes to prevent over-browning. Serve warm. If candy sprinkles are not used, try drizzling a thin powdered sugar icing over bread while warm.

BROILED EASTER EGG SANDWICH

- *Use up those hard-cooked eggs.*

1 c. grated mild cheddar cheese
1 1/2 tsp. onion, minced
1/3 c. sweet pickle, chopped
1 hard-cooked egg, chopped

1/4 tsp. worcestershire sauce
1/8 tsp. salt
1/4 c. mayonnaise
4 slices of bread

Combine cheese, onion, pickle, egg, worcestershire sauce, salt, and mayonnaise. Mix together and spread on plain or toasted bread. Place sandwiches under the broiler until cheese melts. Makes 4 open face sandwiches.

BUNNY COOKIES

- *Sweet bunnies to fill a basket.*

    Peanut-shaped sandwich cookies
    Vanilla flavored almond bark
    Candy-coated fun chips
    Flavored fruit leather roll
    Miniature marshmallows
    Colored icing

Melt almond bark in the microwave or in a double boiler. Dip each cookie in the melted almond bark and place on waxed paper. Immediately, before coating has time to set, place candy-coated fun chips on one end of the cookie to make the eyes and nose. Cut two oval ear shapes out of the fruit leather roll (or cut from paper) and insert at the top of the cookie. Let cookie set until coating is firm. Make three whiskers on either side of the nose using colored icing (or melted chocolate chips), in a pastry bag with a small round tip. Attach a miniature marshmallow on the back of the cookie for a tail. Place bunnies in a basket filled with green-tinted coconut and use as an "edible" centerpiece.

PRETTY PARTY MINTS

- *Melt-in-your-mouth mints.*

3 c. powdered sugar	Mix together powdered sugar and cream cheese to form a pliable dough. Adjust amounts of powdered sugar if needed. Add flavoring and food coloring of your choice. Shape dough like small eggs and roll into granulated sugar or roll small balls into granulated sugar then flatten with a fork.
3-oz. cream cheese	
Oil flavoring	
Food coloring	
Granulated sugar	

COCONUT ALMOND EGGS

- *The Easter bunny will want to fill his own basket with these eggs!*

    1 can (14 oz.) sweetened condensed milk
    1 envelope unflavored gelatin
    1 pkg. (14 oz.) flaked coconut
    Whole almonds
    Dipping chocolate

Place sweetened condensed milk and gelatin in a saucepan and bring to a boil over medium heat, stirring constantly. Remove from heat and stir in coconut. Cool slightly. Mold the coconut mixture into small egg shapes and place on a waxed paper lined cookie sheet. Place an almond on top of each coconut egg. Melt chocolate in a double boiler over low heat. Dip each egg into the chocolate to coat and place on waxed paper. Refrigerate until chocolate is firm.

JELLY BEAN NEST COOKIES

- *Jelly bean eggs nestle in a green coconut nest.*

1 c. butter or margarine
1 pkg. (8 oz.) cream cheese
2 c. granulated sugar
1 egg
1 tsp. vanilla
1/4 tsp. coconut extract

1/4 tsp. almond extract
1 tsp. baking powder
3 1/2 c. flour
Flaked coconut (tinted green)
Jelly beans

Beat together margarine and cream cheese. Add sugar, egg, vanilla, coconut, and almond extracts. Mix well. In a separate bowl sift together flour and baking powder. Gradually add flour mixture to the creamed ingredients, beating well after each addition.

Drop tablespoons of dough onto a lightly greased cookie sheet. Bake at 350 degrees for 12 minutes. Cookies will not brown on top but will remain a creamy white color. Remove from oven and immediately scoop the top out of each cookie. Fill the top of each cookie with tinted coconut to make a nest and place 3 candy jelly beans in each. (To tint coconut, place coconut in a plastic bag with several drops of green food coloring and shake to coat.)

Note: To use this recipe when it is not the Easter holiday, omit coconut and jelly beans and stir a 12 ounce package of chocolate chips into the dough. Makes great chocolate chip cookies.

EASTER LILY CONES

- *Rolled cookies filled with sweetened whipped cream.*

3 eggs
2/3 c. granulated sugar
1/4 tsp. lemon extract
1/4 c. cold water
1 c. flour
1/2 tsp. baking powder
1/4 tsp. salt
Sweetened whipped cream

Separate eggs. Beat yolks until thick and lemon colored. Gradually add sugar, lemon extract, and water. Mix well. Sift together dry ingredients and add to the egg mixture. Whip egg whites until stiff peaks form. Fold egg whites into egg yolk mixture. Grease and flour a cookie sheet. Drop batter by spoonfuls onto the cookie sheet. Spread batter into 6" circles with the back of the spoon. Bake at 375 degrees until edges are golden brown. When done, remove from oven and **quickly** shape cookies into cone shapes. Hold cookies until cone shapes are set. When ready to serve, fill with sweetened whipped cream. Yield 20 cones. *Note:* Wash cookie sheet after each batch of cookies. Grease and flour each time cookies are baked to prevent sticking.

DECORATE A LOVELY EASTER TABLE

- *Spring into spring with these table setting ideas.*

Dinner Nest
Place a "nest" of shredded paper Easter grass under each dinner or salad plate on your Easter table. This will make the table casual or elegant depending on the type of grass or other decor used.

Easter Egg Place Cards
At each place setting, use dyed eggs as place cards. Simply dye hard cooked eggs a bright or pastel color. Using a silver or gold marker write the name of each guest on the egg. Place at each setting in egg cups. Inexpensive wooden napkin rings can be purchased at craft stores that also work great to hold the eggs. Paint to coordinate with the eggs.

Tulle Tablecloth
Cover a white tablecloth with pastel colored tulle (net). This makes a beautiful spring look and is inexpensive. At each corner of the table, tulle can be gathered and tied with a ribbon and bow.

Spring Napkin Rings
Using a thread and needle, carefully string candy **jelly beans**. Make each strand long enough to wrap around a napkin several times. Securely tie ends together and place napkin through.

Wrap napkins with a large **pastel colored bow** and tuck in a fresh cut daffodil or other spring flower.

Place napkins through a **candy necklace**. These can be purchased in pastel colors and are on elastic so can be wrapped around a napkin several times.

Easter Candy Centerpiece
Purchase novelty candies on a stick or some that can be wired onto a florist pick or wooden skewer. Use candies such as wrapped chocolate bunnies, large round colorful lollipops, candy sticks, etc. Place a piece of floral foam in a basket and make an arrangement with the different candies in the foam. Try to obtain a unique assortment of candies to make this a really fun centerpiece.

Pastel Placemats
Cut placemat-sized pieces of pastel colored tissue paper. Crinkle each piece into a ball and then smooth out. Place one under each plate and tie each set of silverware with a coordinating color of satin ribbon or tulle (net). Placemats are very spring looking and are also disposable.

Balloon Bouquets
For a pretty spring centerpiece, purchase a bouquet of pastel colored helium balloons. Place a rock in the bottom of a small white or pastel colored lunch sack. Decorate sack if desired. Tie balloons to the rock. Gather the top of the sack and tie with curling ribbon. Colored cellophane can also be wrapped around a rock as an anchor for the balloons. Sprinkle egg-shaped confetti and jelly bean candies down the center of the table.

TEACUP CENTERPIECES

• *Drink to this idea!*

Throughout the year, shop at thrift stores and yard sales to collect one-of-a-kind teacups and saucers. Use the teacups and the following ideas to make lovely spring centerpieces.

Fresh Flower Teacups
Fill teacups with a small amount of potting soil and pot flowers in bloom (pansies, daffodils, tulips, narcissus, hyacinth, etc.). Tie a ribbon around the base of the flower stems or press sheet moss on top of soil if desired. Place teacups on saucers and randomly place down center of table. Place ribbons and small foil-wrapped candies among the cups for accent.

Waxed Blossom Centerpieces
Dip the blossoms of fresh cut flowers (or greenery) into melted paraffin wax. Place on waxed paper and allow to harden. Arrange in teacups with blossom heads peeking out. Make several and place down the center of a table. Waxed blossoms in teacups also make a nice display at each place setting.

Teacup Candle Centerpieces
Fill pretty teacups with colored paraffin wax. Place wicks in the center of the teacups before adding the wax by tying candle wicking to flat wooden sticks and placing across the top of the teacups. Fill each teacup with melted paraffin wax. (Add color by melting a crayon with paraffin.) When wax is set, remove sticks and trim wicks to desired lengths.

MUFFIN TIN GIFT

• *A fun way to wish someone a happy Easter.*

Purchase a muffin tin with either large or small cups. Fill each muffin cup with a tiny amount of Easter grass. Fill each cup with a different type of Easter candy such as candy kisses, foil-covered eggs, marshmallow bunnies, chocolate coins, jelly beans, etc. Use a variety of candies and make it colorful and creative! Wrap with clear or pastel cellophane and add a bow. Great for any holiday, just omit the Easter grass.

MARBLEIZED BASKETS

• *Make an old basket look like new.*

Use this technique to add some life to an old basket. A paint and water mixture will create a marbleized look on your project. Flat woven baskets tend to work best but anything with a hard smooth surface, including paper, will work. To marbleize a basket, fill a bucket with water. Stir the water to create a whirling motion. Spray the whirling water with two different colors of spray paint. Immediately dip the basket or other item into the swirling water and quickly remove. Let dry.

DELICIOUS SPRING FLOWERS

- *Dress up foods with an array of blossoms.*

Gumdrop Flowers
Roll out soft gumdrops on a flat surface sprinkled with granulated sugar. Roll up a gumdrop piece into a tight cone to form the center of a rose. Wrap additional gumdrop pieces around the cone to form rose petals. Continue adding gumdrop petals until rose is of desired size. Squeeze bottom, pinch pieces together, and trim if necessary. Use green gumdrops for leaves. Other flowers can also be made using gumdrops.

Sugared Flowers
Use non-toxic, pesticide free blossoms such as pansies, rose petals, carnations, daisies, lilacs, bachelor's buttons, honeysuckle, impatiens, and violets. (Many flowers are edible, but don't eat them if in doubt!) Beat an egg white until frothy. Using fingers or a pastry brush, brush egg white onto the flower blossoms coating all sides. Sprinkle blossoms with granulated sugar and gently tap off excess. Place blossoms onto a waxed paper lined cookie sheet. Let dry for 24 hours. Use flowers to decorate cakes and other pastries. Non-toxic leaves can also be sugared and used to accent the sugared blossoms.

Marshmallow Flowers
To make marshmallow flowers, cut across the flat side of a large marshmallow making 3-4 slices. Dip the sticky marshmallow exposed on each piece into pastel colored sugar to coat. Colors that look nice are yellow, pink, and lavender. This will form the petals. Arrange 5 pieces together in a circle to form a daisy-shaped flower. Dip several cut marshmallows in green sugar to make leaves. Make the center of the flowers by using half of a miniature marshmallow or gumdrop.

Beautiful Butter Buds
Place chilled butter into a pastry bag with a rose-making tip. Squeeze butter into rosebud shapes on a waxed paper lined tray. Freeze until firm. Remove butter rosebuds from the freezer just before serving. Use to garnish vegetables, pancakes, meats, or bread.

FLOWER POT DESSERT

- *Make a flower pot of ice cream for each guest. Great for a spring brunch.*

Fill paper cups with softened ice cream or line an unglazed clay or plastic flower pot with foil and fill with ice cream. (Don't allow ice cream to come in contact with clay pots.) Sprinkle the ice cream with crushed chocolate cookies to resemble dirt. Freeze until firm. Make a small hole in the center of the ice cream and insert a flower before serving. Use a paper flower on a wood skewer, a silk flower, or a large lollipop.

This is also a fun idea for a Mother's Day luncheon. Have each child paint a flower pot for their mother and serve the dessert in it. The flower pot would be unique and a special keepsake for each mother.

CHICKEN FEED

- *Your little chicks will love this snack!*

    1 lb. bag of M&M brand candies
    3 c. miniature marshmallows
    1 small box fruit ring cereal
    1 c. raisins
    1 c. small pretzels
    1 can (16 oz.) dry roasted peanuts

Mix together all ingredients. This makes a great snack for the kids. Bag some up and tie with a ribbon for a fun Easter basket filler. Try serving in ice cream cones for variety.

BUNNY BISCUITS

- *Kids love these biscuits shaped like bunnies.*

Make your favorite biscuit dough (or purchase refrigerator biscuits). Cut two circles with a biscuit cutter. Cut one circle in half and press each piece onto the top of the round biscuit to make ears. Draw on features using a toothpick and food coloring. Bake until golden.

CUPCAKE WALK

- *The last child standing on an egg wins the grand prize.*

Cut large, brightly colored egg-shapes from cardstock and number each egg. Make one egg per child playing the game. Write corresponding numbers on small pieces of paper and place in a bowl. Tape the eggs in a circle on the floor. Have each child stand on a numbered egg. Play some music and instruct the children to walk in a circle on the eggs and stop when the music stops. Draw a number out of the bowl each time you stop the music. Give the child standing on that number a cupcake and eliminate that child and numbered egg from the game. Continue until there is only one egg and one child left. Give the remaining child an entire cake or a basket filled with treats.

Place a row of peeled, hard-cooked eggs inside a meatloaf. Bake as usual. A great way to use up some of those leftover Easter eggs.

CHOCOLATE RASPBERRY TRUFFLE EGGS

- *For real chocolate lovers only!*

      8-oz. dipping chocolate or semi-sweet summer coating
      6 large eggs

Using the tip of a sharp knife, gently make a hole at each end of 6 raw eggs. Break away shell on one end of each egg to make a hole approximately the size of your little finger. Blow out the insides of the eggs through the large holes. Place the hollow eggshells in a saucepan and cover with water. Make sure eggshells fill with the water and are completely covered. Bring to a gentle boil and simmer uncovered for 20 minutes. This will sterilize the shells. Remove from water and drain. Shake each shell to drain water and any remaining egg white. Gently rinse in cool water. Let shells dry at least 24 hours before filling.

Place a piece of tape over the small hole in the end of each egg. Place shells in egg carton with the large hole up. Melt chocolate in a double boiler. Place chocolate in a pastry bag with a small round tip and pipe approximately 2 tablespoons of chocolate into each egg. Gently roll each shell to completely coat interior with the chocolate. Shake any excess out through the large hole. Allow to set in refrigerator for at least one hour.

Filling
      1 pkg. (8 oz.) cream cheese
      1 c. semi-sweet chocolate chips
      1/3 c. seedless raspberry jam
      1/4 c. powdered sugar

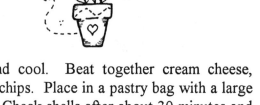

To make filling, melt chocolate chips in a double boiler and cool. Beat together cream cheese, powdered sugar, and raspberry jam. Beat in melted chocolate chips. Place in a pastry bag with a large round tip. Completely fill the eggs with the truffle filling mix. Check shells after about 30 minutes and fill to top if settling has occurred. Chill for several hours. Remove tape from shells, peel, and serve.

JUICY JELLIES

- *Cut Easter shapes from this juice flavored gelatin. A great snack for the kids.*

      4 envelopes unflavored gelatin
      1 1/4 c. cold water
      1 can (6 oz.) frozen juice concentrate, thawed

Sprinkle gelatin over water in a medium-sized saucepan. Stir over low heat until gelatin is completely dissolved. Remove from heat and stir in juice. Pour into a 9" x 9" pan and chill. When firm, cut into Easter shapes using cookie cutters. Juicy Jellies can also be cut into cubes.

EASTER CHICK

- *Serve these hard-cooked little chicks Easter morning.*

Peel a hard-cooked egg and cut the white in half being careful not to cut the yolk. The yolk becomes the head of the chick as it is setting in its nest. Use a tip of a pointed toothpick for the nose or a piece of a carrot shaped to a point. For eyes you can use raisins or small pieces of other vegetables cut to size. To be extra creative, scallop or make pie-shaped cuts around the white part of the egg. These little chicks are great served Easter morning and help use up some of those hard-cooked eggs.

Dust purchased chocolate eggs and bunnies with cocoa powder to give them a truffle like coating!

NATURAL EGG DYES

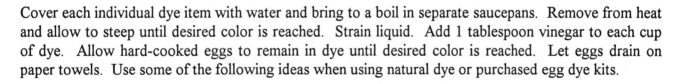

- *Natural dyes make unique Easter eggs.*

    Red – beets
    Orange – onion skins
    Brown – coffee, walnut shells
    Blue – red cabbage leaves, blueberries
    Green – mint leaves, carrot greens, celery tops
    Violet – cranberries, concord grapes, red cabbage mixed with beets
    Yellow – yellow onion skins, celery tops, carrot tops, orange peels, saffron, dandelion blossoms

Cover each individual dye item with water and bring to a boil in separate saucepans. Remove from heat and allow to steep until desired color is reached. Strain liquid. Add 1 tablespoon vinegar to each cup of dye. Allow hard-cooked eggs to remain in dye until desired color is reached. Let eggs drain on paper towels. Use some of the following ideas when using natural dye or purchased egg dye kits.

1. Cook eggs with 1 tablespoon of vinegar added to the water. Shells of the hard-cooked eggs will soften and dye will take better.
2. Add 1 teaspoon of vegetable oil to each cup of dye and eggs will appear marbled after dipping.
3. Wrap eggs with elastic bands before placing in dye.
4. Place small stickers or pieces of tape on egg before placing in dye.
5. Add salt to the water when cooking eggs and they will peel much better.

PASTEL COOKIE DOUGH

- *Pretty spring sugar cookies.*

Make your favorite sugar cookie dough recipe (or use the recipe in the Valentine's Day section of this book.) Divide the dough into several portions. Using food coloring, knead a different color into each portion. Pastel colors look nice for Easter but bright rainbow colors are also a lot of fun. Use dough to make cut-out cookies.

Bunny Cookies
When making cut-out sugar cookies try this. Make a fist and open your first and second fingers to form a "V" shape. Trace around hand and fingers to create a pattern for a bunny head and ears. Makes cute cookies and is a lot of fun for children.

Cookie Lollipops
Make cut-out sugar cookies in Easter shapes such as eggs, bunnies, and tulips. Place a wooden stick under each cookie and press the dough down to adhere to stick. Bake the cookies and decorate with pastel icing and candies. Place a piece of florist foam in a basket and cover with Easter grass. Press the stick of each cookie into the foam. Use as a centerpiece.

EASTER HAT COOKIES

- *Dress up your spring table with these edible bonnets.*

Purchase round (3" - 4" in diameter), scalloped-edged sugar cookies and large, pastel or white colored marshmallows. With icing, attach a large marshmallow to the center of each cookie. Place a narrow ribbon around the base of the marshmallow and tie a bow. Add tiny icing or silk flowers around the "brim" of the cookie hat.

SHORTCAKE BASKETS

- *A treat made from purchased cakes.*

Purchase individual shortcake cups. Frost sides of the cakes with white icing. Press white, yellow, or pink-tinted coconut (tint by placing several drops of food coloring in a plastic bag with the shredded coconut and shake) onto the icing to cover sides. Sprinkle green-tinted coconut in the center for "grass." Bend a pipe cleaner and push it down into the rim of the cake on either side to make a handle. Fill with jelly beans and other small Easter candies.

EASTER BONNET PARADE

- *Let children create a fashion parade.*

Place a variety of items such as paper plates, ribbons, silk flowers, tissue paper, buttons, glue, scissors, etc. on a large table. Help children make creative Easter bonnets or hats using the items. Let the children dress up in fancy dresses, gloves, parasols, etc. and wear their homemade bonnets. Have an Easter parade and invite parents to watch. March the parade around the house or around the neighborhood. Take lots of pictures!

SWEET DOUGH BUNNIES

- *Hop hoppity good!*

    1 Tbs. active dry yeast
    1/4 c. lukewarm water
    1/2 c. milk, scalded
    1/2 c. margarine
    1/2 c. granulated sugar
    1 tsp. salt
    2 eggs
    1-2 Tbs. grated orange zest
    1/4 c. orange juice
    4-4 1/2 c. flour

Place yeast in warm water. Set aside. Scald milk and add margarine, sugar, and salt. Stir until margarine is melted and mixture is lukewarm. Add yeast mixture, eggs, orange zest, orange juice, and enough flour to make a soft dough. Knead until smooth and elastic. Place in a greased bowl and cover. Let rise until double. Punch down dough and use to make sweet dough bunnies or bread dough nests.

Bunnies

To make each bunny, roll a piece of dough into a 14" x 1/2" rope. Cross ends of rope to make a circle at the bottom. Bring the underneath piece up over the top leaving ends spread open to make "ears" (see illustration). Pinch ends of dough to make pointed "ears." Roll a small 1" ball of dough and place in center of circle to form a "tail." Place on a greased cookie sheet and let rise until doubled. Bake at 375 degrees for 10-15 minutes. Bunnies can be frosted with a powdered sugar glaze while warm.

Bread Dough Nest

To make a bread dough nest, shape 1/3 of a batch of the above sweet dough recipe into 6 small egg shapes. Place the balls in the center of a greased cookie sheet, with sides touching. With remaining dough, form two 25" long ropes and twist together. Place around the dough eggs and pinch ends together. This should look like eggs sitting in a nest. Cover and let rise until doubled. Bake at 375 degrees for 15-20 minutes. Cool and remove from cookie sheet.

Using a thin powdered sugar icing, frost each bread egg. Sprinkle a different color of colored sugar on each frosted egg or decorate with a variety of small candy sprinkles or small candies. Each egg should be different. Frost bread ropes around outside of bread eggs and cover with green-tinted coconut if desired. This colorful bread nest is pretty enough to be served for Easter dinner.

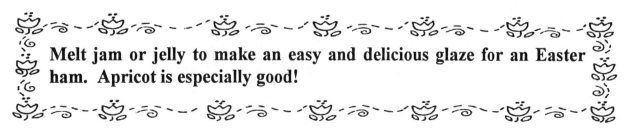

Melt jam or jelly to make an easy and delicious glaze for an Easter ham. Apricot is especially good!

PASTEL FLOWER POTS

- *Real grass grows from these centerpieces.*

Purchase several small sizes of clay flower pots. Using acrylic paints, paint all the pots with an ivory or cream color paint. Paint each rim a different pastel color such as yellow, pink, or lavender. Cut Easter shapes out of a clean kitchen or craft sponge (tulips, eggs, or bunnies) and sponge-paint shapes around the bottom of each pot. Wrap a ribbon around each pot and add a bow.

Fill each pot with potting soil and sprinkle with grass or wheat seed. Lightly cover with dirt, sprinkle with water, and keep in a sunny place. Grass should grow within several weeks. Trim grass as needed.

PAPIER-MÂCHÉ EGG PIÑATAS

- *Filled with Easter candy, this egg will be the "hit" of the party!*

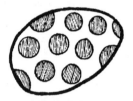

Paste   4 c. water
1/2 c. flour
4 Tbs. granulated sugar

In a saucepan, combine flour and water and mix until smooth. Bring to a boil. Remove from heat and stir in sugar. Let cool. Once mixture is cool and has thickened, it is ready to use.

Blow up a large 14" - 16" balloon. Tie a knot securely in the end. Tear numerous 1" strips from newspaper. Dip strips in the paste and squeeze off excess paste with fingers. Place strips onto the balloon. Continue to add strips overlapping them as you cover the entire balloon. Let dry overnight.

When first layer is dry, wrap a string around the balloon and tie a loop at the top. Add a second and third layer of newspaper strips covering the balloon and string in the same manner as the first. (Leave the loop of the string exposed to form the hanger.) Dry between each layer and be careful to make the layers even.

When third layer is dry, paint piñata or decorate with fringed tissue paper to look like an Easter egg. Cut a small door at one end of the balloon. Pop the balloon and make sure interior of piñata is dry.

Fill the egg piñata with wrapped candies and unbreakable trinkets. Tape door closed. Suspend from a pole and raise up and down as children try to hit the piñata with a plastic bat. Provide the children with small baskets or sacks for gathering candy when the piñata breaks.

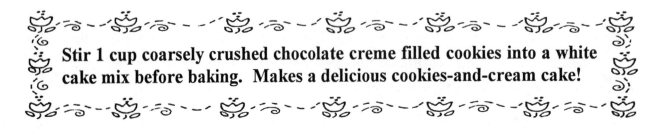

Stir 1 cup coarsely crushed chocolate creme filled cookies into a white cake mix before baking. Makes a delicious cookies-and-cream cake!

THE GREAT EGG HUNT

- *Add some variety to your annual Easter egg hunt.*

Color-Coded Egg Hunt
Dye hard-cooked eggs with bright colors (paste food coloring in 1 cup water plus 1/4 cup vinegar makes vivid colored eggs). Hide the eggs and assign each age group of children a certain color to find. Make sure to hide eggs so even the youngest children can find them easily. (Assign each child a color to find if there are just a few children going on the hunt.) The children may only keep their assigned color even if other eggs are found. This is a great way to make sure everyone has eggs to take home.

Treasure Egg Hunt
Create a treasure hunt hiding the clues in plastic Easter eggs. Make sure to have a big basket of goodies at the end of the hunt.

Redeemable Egg Hunt
Sort plastic eggs into colors. Purchase small novelty items, small packaged nutritious treats, toys, etc. and assign each type of item to a color of egg. Choose one color of egg to be the grand prize or have a grand prize egg for each child. Hide the empty eggs, and when the children have finished the hunt, eggs can be redeemed. Each color of egg will be given a certain prize. Make the grand prize something fun!

Raw Egg Hunt
Dye numerous hard-cooked eggs and one raw egg. Hide the dyed eggs around the yard. When time for the egg hunt, give the children baskets or other containers filled with Easter grass for collecting the eggs. When all the eggs have been found, instruct the children to gently crack their eggs. (Be prepared to make deviled eggs!) What a fun surprise a child will have as he/she finds the raw egg! Award the child with the raw egg a special prize.

CANDLE EGGS

- *Real eggshells make the molds for these unique candles.*

Make a pinhole in each end of a raw egg. Make one hole about 3/8 " in diameter by gently breaking the egg shell. Break the yolk by inserting a toothpick and gently blow out the insides of the egg. Rinse and let dry. Place a small piece of masking tape over the small hole and place egg in an egg carton with the large hole up. Melt a brick of paraffin wax in an old can placed in a pan of warm water over low heat. Melt a crayon with the paraffin to create the desired color. Pour a small amount of wax in the egg and wait several seconds to make sure the bottom hole is sealed. Fill the entire egg shell full of wax. Place a 3" piece of candle wicking in the hole, leaving the end exposed. Allow wax to harden. Peel shell off and gently scrape bottom to create a flat area so egg won't tip.

To make **half-shell candles**, carefully break an egg in half. Try to keep the two eggshell halves as intact as possible. Rinse. Dye the half-shells in egg dye and let air dry thoroughly. Place half-shells in an egg carton. Place a 4" piece of candle wicking in the center of each half-shell. Pour melted paraffin wax in each shell. (Wax can be tinted to match shells by adding crayons to hot wax.) Let wax harden and trim wicks. Place in egg holders and use at each place setting or as a centerpiece.

NOODLE NESTS

- *A crunchy, chocolate nest that holds pretty jelly bean eggs.*

Melt 2 cups semi-sweet chocolate chips over low heat in a double boiler. Stir in 2 cups dry chow mien noodles until coated with chocolate. Drop by tablespoonfuls onto waxed paper and using a spoon make an indention in the center to form a nest. Let set and place several small jelly beans inside the chocolate nest. These cute nests can be placed on cupcakes or other Easter desserts.

POPCORN BASKET

- *An edible basket that "pops" with character!*

    1 c. light corn syrup
    1/2 c. granulated sugar
    1 small pkg. (3 oz.) flavored gelatin
    2 1/2 qts. popped popcorn

Bring corn syrup and sugar to a boil. Add gelatin and stir constantly until gelatin is dissolved completely. Pour over popcorn and stir to coat well. Press into a well greased mixing bowl and press to make popcorn approximately 1" thick on bottom and sides of the bowl. To form a handle, make a rope of popcorn and curve to fit basket. Set on waxed paper and let set in refrigerator. When set, remove popcorn from mixing bowl and attach handle with Royal Icing (see page 102).

LOVE BASKET

- *Fill eggs with gifts of love and time.*

Fill a basket with plastic eggs. Inside each egg place a "coupon" that the recipient can redeem in the following months. Coupons could be for a walk in the park, a new book, an ice cream cone, no chores on a certain day, a favorite dinner fixed, a night out to the movies, etc...

SPRINGTIME CAKE

- *Create unique cake flavors and colors.*

To create a pretty springtime cake, simply use a white cake mix and stir in a package of dry flavored gelatin. Save a small amount of gelatin to add to the frosting. This will give the frosting the same color and flavor as the cake. Cake can also be topped with flaked coconut that has been tinted and flavored with dry flavored gelatin mix.

FOURTH OF JULY

SPARKLER STICKS

- *Red, white, and blue candy sprinkles top these chocolate coated pretzel rods. Great for munching!*

    Large pretzel rods
    Dipping chocolate
    Vanilla flavored almond bark
    Red, white, and blue candy sprinkle mix
    Red and blue curling ribbon

Melt dipping chocolate and vanilla flavored almond bark in separate double boilers. Dip half of each pretzel rod into the dipping chocolate and let set on waxed paper. Place in freezer until chocolate is firm. When set, quickly dip chocolate covered end of the pretzel rod into the melted almond bark, coating half of the dipping chocolate. Immediately roll in the candy sprinkles and let set until firm. Wrap curling ribbon around the lower half of the pretzel rod and curl. Place containers of these "sparkler sticks" on your picnic or holiday table for munching. Makes a great decoration as well as a festive treat.

WATERMELON CAKE

- *A pink cake with chocolate chip "seeds" and a green coconut "rind."*

Mix together a pink-colored cake mix (or add red food coloring to a white cake mix) according to package directions. Sprinkle miniature chocolate chips into the batter before baking. The chocolate chips will resemble watermelon seeds. Bake in two 8" round cake pans. When cake has cooled, ice the bottom layer with pink-tinted icing (watermelon color). Add the top layer and also spread with the pink icing. Score icing on top of cake into 8 wedges. Spread sides and top outer edge (1") of cake with white icing. Press green-tinted coconut onto the white icing covering it to resemble a watermelon rind. Place several chocolate chips on top of the cake. Cut in wedges to serve. *Note:* Cake can be baked in a 9" x 13" cake pan. Frost entire top with white icing and cover with green-tinted coconut or green-tinted sugar. Cut into squares to serve.

ICE CREAM BROWNIE CONES

- *Bake a brownie surprise in an ice cream cone.*

Make your favorite brownie recipe. Fill ice cream cones 2/3 full with brownie batter. Place cones standing up on a cookie sheet and bake for 20 minutes or until a toothpick inserted comes out clean. Let cool. Place a scoop of ice cream on the cones and sprinkle with small candies.

BETSY ROSS CAKE

- *A red, white, and blue cake that would make Betsy Ross proud.*

Make a white cake. Divide batter into three bowls. Tint batter in one bowl with red food coloring, one with blue food coloring, and the third leave untinted. Spoon the colored batters next to each other into a greased and floured 9" x 13" cake pan. Alternate batters until cake pan is filled and there is no batter remaining. Gently take a knife and swirl through batter once. Bake as directed. (An angel food cake mix also works for this recipe. Bake in an angel food cake pan for best results.)

FIRECRACKER CAKES

- *Cakes baked in soup cans make an explosive statement!*

Generously grease and flour an empty, clean soup can. Make a cake from scratch or use cake batter from a purchased cake mix. Fill the soup can 2/3 full of batter. Bake as directed. Test for doneness as this may take a little longer than a cupcake to bake. Remove from oven and cool slightly. Carefully loosen edges of cake with a knife. (You can also remove the bottom of the can and push the loose lid though the can forcing the cake out the other end.) Decorate sides of cake with red frosting and white frosting on the top making it look like a firecracker. Place a piece of chenille stem or foil sparkler in the top to make a fuse.

LAYERED ICE CREAM BALLS

- *Dig into this dessert at the end of a hot summer day.*

Roll large scoops of vanilla ice cream into balls and wrap individually in plastic wrap. Place in freezer until frozen. Remove from freezer and roll each ball in a topping such as red and blue candy sprinkles, nuts, crushed candy bars, chocolate chips, cookie chunks, coconut, etc. Serve immediately.

STAR-SPANGLED STRAWBERRIES

- *Chocolate dipped strawberries dressed in patriotic colors.*

Wash and pat dry large, firm strawberries. Dip one side of each strawberry in either melted semi-sweet dipping chocolate or vanilla flavored almond bark. Immediately roll coated side of strawberry in chopped nuts, coconut, or red, white, and blue candy sprinkles. Eat as a snack or serve on top of ice cream or cake.

APPLE STACKS

- *Layer apple slices and filling to make a nutritious summer snack.*

Wash and core red apples. Cut crosswise into 3 or 4 thick slices. Spread each slice with peanut butter or strawberry-flavored cream cheese. Stack slices back together to form an apple shape. To make a colorful stack, alternate red and green apple slices.

CITRUS CUPS

- *Light and refreshing treats for a hot July day.*

Cut the tops off lemons, oranges, or limes. Carefully scoop out the inside fruit so rind forms a cup. Fill the citrus shells with scoops of matching sorbets or sherbets. Wrap in plastic wrap and freeze. Makes a pretty dessert!

WATERMELON DESSERT

- *Raspberry sherbet and chocolate chips make a watermelon look-alike!*

Cut a watermelon in half length-wise. Scoop watermelon fruit, leaving a rind bowl. (Use watermelon fruit for a salad.) Soften approximately 1/2 gallon of dark pink raspberry sherbet and stir in 2 cups chocolate chips. Spoon sherbet into melon rind and smooth even with top. Sprinkle a few chocolate chips on top around edges and press into sherbet to look like seeds. Freeze until firm. Use a scoop to serve or slice.

For a quick and refreshing fruit dip, combine 8 ounces cream cheese and 14 ounces marshmallow creme. Blend well and chill.

RED, WHITE, AND BLUE BREAKFAST BAR

- *Let your family build their own red, white, and blue breakfast.*

Spend a morning together as a family and enjoy a wonderful holiday breakfast! Prepare waffles, crepes, French toast, or pancakes. French toast or pancakes can be cut into star shapes by using a large cookie cutter. Set the breakfast table with berries and toppings that are red, white, and blue, such as strawberries, blueberries, raspberries, whipped cream, powdered sugar, raspberry syrup, and strawberry jam. Have family members assemble their own patriotic breakfast.

INDEPENDENCE DAY PARFAITS

- *A perfect dessert to serve in celebration of our country.*

Make a package of blue gelatin and refrigerate until firm. In a separate pan, make and set a package of red gelatin. When gelatin is set, cut into medium size cubes. In individual parfait glasses or a large trifle bowl, assemble dessert by alternating layers of colored gelatin cubes, whipped topping, cubes of pound cake or angel food cake, strawberries, blueberries, and/or raspberries.

PATRIOTIC POPCORN

- *Take a bowl of this colorful popcorn to the parade.*

    1 small pkg. (3 oz.) flavored gelatin (cherry, raspberry, or strawberry
            for red color, or berry blue for blue)
    1 c. granulated sugar
    1 c. light corn syrup
    6-8 qts. popped popcorn

Combine first three ingredients and stir over low heat. Boil for one minute and pour over popped popcorn. Make into balls if desired. For a special surprise, wrap small novelty items in plastic wrap and place inside a large popcorn ball. Another fun idea is to make a batch of each color of popcorn (blue and red) and toss together to create a colorful Fourth of July treat.

FROZEN FLOWERS

- *Icy blossoms to freshen summer beverages.*

To make attractive ice cubes for summer beverages, place small, fresh, non-toxic flower blossoms in each section of an ice cube tray. Cover blossoms with water and freeze. Serve in glasses of clear soda or light colored drinks. A clever touch your guests will not forget!

FROZEN ICE POPS

- *Fill your freezer full of these frosty treats.*

  1 small pkg. (3 oz.) flavored gelatin,
      (any flavor)
  1 pkg. unsweetened flavored drink mix,
      (any flavor)
  1/2 c. granulated sugar
  2 c. cold water
  2 c. hot water

Combine gelatin, sugar, and drink mix. Pour hot water over mixture and stir until ingredients are dissolved. Add cold water and pour into freezer pop molds, small paper cups, or ice cube trays. Freeze. When partially frozen, place wooden sticks in the mixture. Sticks can also be added before freezing by covering molds or cups with a piece of paper and inserting a wooden stick through a slit in the center of the paper. Cover ice cube trays with foil and insert a toothpick into each cube before freezing.

"BERRY GOOD" ICE CREAM

- *A creamy, refreshing treat.*

  2 c. granulated sugar
  1/2 c. lemon juice
  2/3 c. orange juice
  4 c. fresh berries (any combination
      of strawberries, raspberries,
      blueberries, and blackberries)
  1 can (12 oz.) evaporated milk, chilled
  2 c. whipping cream
  2 c. half & half
  1 1/2 tsp. vanilla
  1/4 tsp. salt

Combine sugar, lemon juice, orange juice, and fresh berries. Stir. Whip chilled evaporated milk until fluffy and add to berry mixture. Add half and half, whipping cream, vanilla, and salt. Pour into ice cream freezer. (Add milk, if necessary, to bring mixture to fill line.) Freeze according to manufacturer's directions.

SUMMER DESSERT

- *Quick and easy!*

  1 container (16 oz.) whipped topping
  1/2 gallon rainbow flavored sherbet
  1 pkg. coconut macaroon cookies,
      crushed fine

Mix 3/4 of the whipped topping with all but 1/4 cup crushed cookies. Spread in a 9" x 13" pan. Soften sherbet and spread over macaroon layer. Cover sherbet with the remaining whipped topping and garnish with crushed cookies. Keep frozen until ready to serve.

WATERMELON ICE

- *Serve up scoops of this icy refresher.*

Puree watermelon fruit in a blender to make 3 cups. Mix 2/3 cup granulated sugar, 1 teaspoon grated orange zest, and 1/4 cup orange juice with the watermelon puree. Freeze mixture until almost firm. Break up mixture and beat with an electric mixer until smooth. Do not melt. Place into a shallow pan or bowl and return to freezer until frozen. Remove from freezer several minutes before serving. Using a scoop or a large spoon, scrape up the icy mixture and serve in dessert cups.

CREAM CHEESE STARS

- *Garnish salads and desserts with these creamy stars.*

Sprinkle a cookie sheet with powdered sugar. Spread softened cream cheese 1/4" deep in pan. Chill until firm. Using a small cookie cutter in the shape of a star (or other design), cut stars from cream cheese. To keep cutter from sticking, dip in powdered sugar before cutting the cream cheese.

OLD GLORY ROLL

- *A cake roll filled with berries and cream.*

3 eggs
1 c. granulated sugar
1/3 c. water
1 tsp. vanilla
3/4 c. flour
1 tsp. baking powder
1/4 tsp. salt

Line a jelly roll pan or cookie sheet with waxed paper and grease and flour well. With a mixer, beat eggs on high speed for about 5 minutes. On low speed, gradually add sugar, water, and vanilla to the beaten eggs. Add flour, baking powder, and salt and beat just until batter is smooth. Pour into the lined pan and bake in a 375 degree oven for 10-14 minutes or until light brown. Immediately invert pan onto a clean dish towel that has been sprinkled with powdered sugar. Gently remove waxed paper, roll up cake with the dish towel, and allow to cool.

Filling

1 container (8 oz.) whipped topping
2 Tbs. powdered sugar
2 c. fresh sliced strawberries, or fresh raspberries
1 c. blueberries

Mix together whipped topping and powdered sugar. Unroll cake and spread with the whipped topping mixture. Place the berries over the whipped topping mixture and carefully roll up cake. Sprinkle cake with powdered sugar. Chill. Slice to serve.

COOKIE SALAD

- *Great for a summer barbeque.*

2 small pkgs. (3.4 oz. each) vanilla instant pudding mix
2 c. buttermilk
1 container (12 oz.) whipped topping
1 can (20 oz.) pineapple chunks, drained
2 cans (10 oz. each) mandarin oranges, drained
1/2 pkg. fudge-striped shortbread cookies

Combine pudding mix and buttermilk. Fold in whipped topping. Add drained pineapple and mandarin oranges. Crush cookies into large pieces and fold into mixture immediately before serving. Serve as a salad, a dessert, or as individual parfaits.

JULY CREAM PIE

- *A slice of sheer delight!*

1 pkg. (8 oz.) cream cheese
1/3 c. granulated sugar
1/4 tsp. almond extract
1 container (8 oz.) whipped topping
2 pints strawberries, stemmed
2 c. fresh blueberries, or blueberry pie filling
9" pie shell, baked
1/2 c. semi-sweet chocolate chips
1 Tbs. shortening

Mix together cream cheese, sugar, and almond extract. Blend in whipped topping and mix until smooth. Pour into baked pie shell and chill. Melt chocolate chips with shortening. Dip the pointed end of each strawberry into the chocolate, coating half of each berry. Place on waxed paper and allow to set until chocolate is firm. Arrange strawberries in the center of the pie on the chilled cream filling. Leave a 1" area uncovered around the edge. Sprinkle blueberries on the outside edge of the pie.

PICNIC SANDWICH RING

- *A giant bagel-shaped sandwich that serves a crowd.*

Using purchased or homemade bread dough, divide and make two long ropes. (Sandwich can be made large or small depending on amount of dough used.) Place the ropes together and twist. Invert a small, glass, oven-proof bowl onto the center of a greased cookie sheet and grease bowl well. Wrap the twisted dough ropes around the bowl and pinch ends together. Cover and let rise until doubled. Bake as directed until bread is done. Remove from oven and cool for several minutes. Remove bowl from the center of bread. When cool, slice bread ring horizontally and fill with a variety of cold cuts, cheeses, and other sandwich fillings. Slice to serve.

For a quick sandwich, slice a loaf of French bread horizontally and fill with sandwich fillings. French bread can also be hollowed out and filled with Sloppy Joe or barbeque beef filling. Great for a picnic.

TACO SALAD BOWLS

- *Make your own salad bowls using flour tortillas.*

Place approximately 5" of vegetable oil in a heavy saucepan. Heat oil to 375 degrees. Lay a large flour tortilla shell over top of pan. Using metal tongs, press a clean, empty, vegetable or soup can (remove label) onto the center of shell pressing it into the hot oil. The sides of the flour shell will flute up around the can as it cooks. Hold can down until shell is golden brown. Drain shell on paper towels and fill with salad of your choice.

STAR CROUTONS

- *Use these crunchy stars to top green salads.*

Using a small star-shaped cookie cutter, cut stars from pieces of bread. Place bread stars on a cookie sheet and sprinkle with melted butter and dried herbs or spices. Let dry in a warm oven for several hours. Serve on salads or soups.

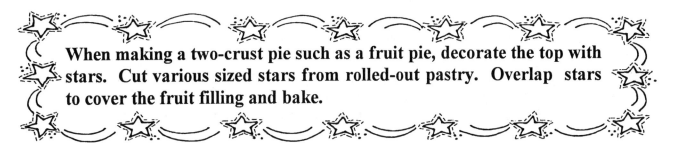

When making a two-crust pie such as a fruit pie, decorate the top with stars. Cut various sized stars from rolled-out pastry. Overlap stars to cover the fruit filling and bake.

SOFT STAR BREAD

- *Top these soft bread stars with a variety of seasonings.*

    1 1/2 c. warm water
    1 Tbs. yeast
    1 Tbs. honey
    1/2 tsp. salt
    1/2 tsp. seasoning salt
    Melted butter
    Grated parmesan cheese, poppy seeds,
        garlic salt, or sesame seeds

Mix together yeast, warm water, and honey. Let set for 5 minutes. Add salt, seasoning salt, and just enough flour to make a soft dough. Roll dough out on a lightly floured surface. Spread with melted butter or margarine and sprinkle with parmesan cheese, poppy seeds, or other topping of your choice. Using a star-shaped cookie cutter (4" - 5" in diameter), cut stars out of the dough and place on a lightly greased cookie sheet. Let rise for 45 minutes and bake at 400 degrees for 12 minutes. Serve with salad or soup. This dough can be cut into simple shapes for any holiday.

SPINACH ALMOND SALAD

- *The best salad you will ever eat! Serve as a complete meal or as a side salad.*

    1 bag (10 oz.) fresh spinach
    3/4 lb. fried bacon, crumbled
    1 c. almond slivers, toasted
    1 Granny Smith apple, sliced very thin

Wash spinach and dry well. Tear into bite sized pieces making sure to remove any large stems. Add bacon, apple, and toasted almonds (toast in a 350 degree oven for 8-10 minutes or until golden brown). Toss with dressing immediately before serving.

Dressing
    1/4 c. granulated sugar
    1/3 c. oil
    1/4 tsp. salt
    1 Tbs. red onion, chopped
    3 Tbs. cider vinegar

Mix ingredients in blender and pour over spinach salad.

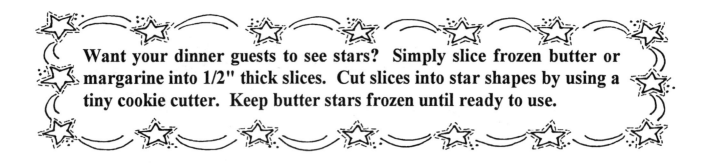

Want your dinner guests to see stars? Simply slice frozen butter or margarine into 1/2" thick slices. Cut slices into star shapes by using a tiny cookie cutter. Keep butter stars frozen until ready to use.

PICNIC PEPPERS

- *Three colors of peppers serve as containers for condiments.*

Purchase a large green, yellow, and red pepper from your local grocery store. Wash each pepper and cut across the top of the pepper to create a "bowl" shape. Carefully hollow out each pepper. Fill the green pepper with relish, the yellow with mustard, and the red with ketchup, and set on a tray ready for your guests to dress up their burgers.

FREEDOM FLOAT

- *Blueberries frozen in ice cubes fill this refreshing treat.*

3 pkgs. cherry-flavored unsweetened powdered drink mix
6 qts. water
2 1/4 c. granulated sugar
1 can (12 oz.) frozen lemonade concentrate
1 can (6 oz.) frozen orange juice concentrate
1 qt. pineapple juice
2 qts. lemon-lime soda
1/2 gallon vanilla ice cream
1 c. blueberries, drained and washed

Mix together powdered drink mix, sugar, and water. Add lemonade and orange juice concentrates. Stir in pineapple juice. Chill. Freeze blueberries in ice cubes. When ready to serve, fill glasses with ice cubes. Pour juice mixture over the ice cubes and add lemon-lime soda to taste. Top each glass with a scoop of ice cream. Garnish with a lemon wedge and a fresh mint sprig. Place a small flag pick in the ice cream. Makes approximately 10 quarts.

COOL, COOL, STRAWBERRY SLUSH

- *A perfect summer heat relief!*

2 pkgs. (any size) frozen strawberries, thawed
1 can (12 oz.) pink lemonade concentrate, thawed
1 c. granulated sugar
5 cans water
Lemon-lime soda
Fresh fruit chunks (opt.)

Mash strawberries with a potato masher. Combine mashed strawberries, lemonade, sugar, and water in a large bowl. Mix well. Pour into a container such as a plastic ice cream bucket. Freeze. To serve, let thaw about one hour. Place a scoop of the slush into each glass and pour lemon-lime soda over the mixture. Thread chunks of fruit on a skewer to make a kabob and use to stir the slush.

BANANA POPS

- *Frozen banana treats that are nutritious and delicious!*

8 large bananas
1 container (8 oz.) whipped topping
16 wooden sticks
Chopped nuts, candy sprinkles, coconut, etc.

Peel bananas and cut in half horizontally. Place a wooden stick in the cut end of each banana piece. Using a knife, carefully spread whipped topping over banana and cover entirely. Roll in chopped nuts, candy sprinkles, or coconut. Place on waxed paper and freeze until firm. Makes 16 banana pops.

EASY SLOPPY JOES

- *A quick meal for a family picnic.*

  1 lb. ground beef
  1 can chicken gumbo soup
  1 onion, chopped
  2 Tbs. ketchup
  2 Tbs. mustard
  Salt and pepper

Brown ground beef and onion. Drain fat. Add soup, ketchup, and mustard. Add salt and pepper to taste. Let simmer and serve on hamburger buns. Serves 8-10. This recipe can be doubled and frozen for future use.

BARBEQUE PICNIC BEANS

- *Take these to the family get-together.*

  10 slices bacon
  1 medium onion, chopped
  1 green bell pepper, chopped
  2 large cans pork and beans
  2 Tbs. dark molasses
  4 tsp. worcestershire sauce
  6 Tbs. brown sugar
  1/4 tsp. oregano
  1 tsp. salt
  Dash pepper

Fry bacon in a skillet. Drain and crumble. Add onion and pepper to the same skillet and cook 5 minutes stirring constantly. Place beans in a casserole dish and mix in crumbled bacon, onion, and pepper mixture and add the remaining ingredients. Bake uncovered in a 375 degree oven for about 1 hour. Serves 10.

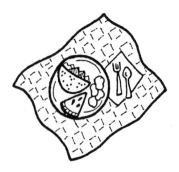

CORN COBLETS

- *Nibble on these small bite-sized corn pieces. Perfect for a picnic.*

Husk fresh ears of corn. Wash and cut ears of corn into 2" segments. Boil in a large pot of water until corn is tender. Drain and serve on a large platter. Serve with butter and salt.

MARVELOUS MARINADE

- *A mouth-watering marinade for grilled poultry.*

  1 c. vegetable oil
  1/2 c. soy sauce
  1/2 c. worcestershire sauce
  3 cloves garlic, minced
  2 c. lemon-lime soda

Mix all ingredients together in a large bowl. Place thawed turkey or chicken in marinade and refrigerate overnight. Grill meat as desired.

STRAWBERRY BITES

- *Strawberries cradle an almond cream filling.*

  1 small pkg. (3.4 oz.) vanilla instant
        pudding mix
  1 c. milk
  1 c. whipping cream, whipped
  3/4 tsp. almond extract
  2 pints large strawberries, stemmed

Mix together pudding mix and milk. Fold in the whipped cream and almond extract. Cut a deep "X" in the pointed end of each berry. Carefully spread apart cut berries to form four connected sections. Place the cream mixture into a pastry bag with a star or other decorative tip. Fill the center of each split berry with the cream mixture. Refrigerate until ready to serve.

LEMONADE SLICE BITES

- *Lemon slices of sweet gelatin.*

    12 large lemons
    1 pkg. unflavored gelatin
    1 1/2 c. cold water
    2/3 c. granulated sugar
    1/2 c. fresh lemon juice

Slice lemons in half length-wise. Carefully remove all pulp from rind, making sure not to put a hole in the rind. Rind should be clean and smooth and resemble a small cup. Place the lemon cups on a baking rack and set onto a cookie sheet.

Add gelatin, water, and sugar in a saucepan and cook over low heat. Stir constantly until gelatin and sugar are dissolved. Stir in lemon juice. Cool mixture. Pour lemon mixture into the lemon rind cups, filling to the brim. Chill cups until gelatin has set. Cut cups in half length-wise forming wedges. Use an electric knife for best results. Use as a garnish or serve as part of a meal. Makes 48 lemon wedges.

A COOL POOL

- *A great way to keep those summer foods and drinks cool!*

Keep food and drinks cool in a pool. Fill a small plastic children's pool with ice. Place bowls of food, watermelons, and canned drinks in the ice. Arrange kale, cabbage, flowers, or balloons in the ice to add color.

Garnish food with stars cut from vegetables such as a red pepper. Sliced starfruit makes a nice addition to fruit salads. Cheese also looks cute cut into stars. Try topping a pizza with cheese stars!

FAMILY T-SHIRTS

- *Unite your family with creative shirts.*

Purchase some inexpensive white T-shirts. Have family members create their own patriotic shirts to wear to the parade and other festivities. Decorate shirts with glitter paints, sequins, ribbons, or fabric markers, or sponge-paint with star-shaped sponges. A great activity for the whole family to enjoy.

FESTIVE FOURTH TABLES

- *Show your patriotism with these red, white, and blue table decor ideas.*

Star Jars
Paint designs, such as stars, with red, white, and blue acrylic paint onto a clean glass jar. Fill jar with flowers, flags, sparklers, or other fun items. Place a ribbon around the top of the jar and tie a bow. Metallic star garland or colored raffia could also be tied around the jar. Use as a centerpiece.

Patriotic Pots
Paint clay pots with red, white, and blue acrylic paint. Sponge-paint stars over the pots using a contrasting color. Let dry and fill with small plants, flags, or bundles of sparklers and use for a centerpiece.

Picnic Rocks
On a windy day, paint small rocks red, white, and blue and use to hold down the tablecloth. Write the name of a guest on each rock to serve as a place card.

Sponge Stars
Cut a clean kitchen or craft sponge into a star shape. Cover picnic table with butcher paper, and using acrylic paint, sponge-paint stars randomly over the paper. Use red, white, and blue paint depending on which color of butcher paper is used.

Firecracker Napkins
Purchase paper or cloth napkins that are solid blue or blue checked. Fold in half and roll napkin. Stand napkins on end and tie a red ribbon around the napkin. Insert red ribbon curls or red paper that has been slit in the top of each napkin to resemble a firecracker fuse.

Summer Bandanas
For a quick inexpensive summer touch, use red or blue cloth bandanas for placemats, napkins, or for basket liners for rolls or bread. Tuck small flags among the rolls in the basket.

Quick Tie-Up
Wrap paper or cloth napkins with a ribbon or a metallic star garland. Tuck a small American flag under the ribbon.

Barbeque Napkins
Use red or blue plaid dishcloths for napkins. These "napkins" are large and very durable and great for the barbeque season. Dishcloth napkins wash well and can be used time and time again.

Flag Favors
Stick tiny American flag picks into large red or white gumdrops and place at each place setting. Fun favors to add holiday spirit!

Patriotic Picnic Baskets
Fill a picnic basket with a flower arrangement and tie on helium balloons and use as a centerpiece. Place tiny woven picnic baskets filled with candies at each place setting for a favor.

PATRIOTIC PAINTING

- *Color the sidewalks with holiday spirit!*

Purchase powdered tempra paint in red, white, and blue. Mix as directed. Give each child an old paintbrush and let them paint flags, stars, etc. on the driveway and sidewalks. Kids will love this and a good rainstorm or a spray with the hose will wash it away.

OLD GLORY GARAGE

- *Turn your garage door into an American flag.*

Decorate your garage door like the American flag. Use brightly colored butcher paper that is available at school and party supply stores for a nominal amount. Make sure to add a sign that says, "Happy Birthday USA!"

HAPPY BIRTHDAY USA!

- *Celebrate by having a fun neighborhood parade.*

Pass flyers around your neighborhood announcing a children's parade is to be held. Inform parents to have their children decorate bikes, wagons, etc. Have two people start the parade with a large banner that states, "HAPPY BIRTHDAY USA." March through your neighborhood (check with your city to obtain permission to use your street or use the sidewalk) for everyone to see. Make sure to have music and lots of flags. Serve patriotic birthday cake and punch at the conclusion of the parade.

HOMEMADE BUBBLES

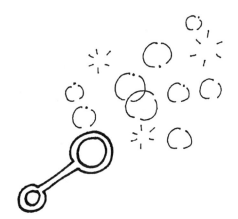

- *Send colorful bubbles high into the sky on a hot summer day.*

  3 c. warm water
  1 c. Dawn brand dish soap
  1/3 c. light corn syrup
  Food coloring (optional)
  Bubble wand (homemade or purchased)

In a bowl, mix water, dish soap, and corn syrup. Drops of food coloring can be added for desired color. Dip a bubble wand into the bubble mixture and blow or move the wand through the air to make bubbles.

To make a **homemade bubble blower**, twist heavy wire (such as a clothes hanger) into a circle, letting part of it be the handle. A long pipe cleaner can also be bent into a wand. Just form a circle and twist together leaving a small part as the handle. Another idea is to cut out the bottom of a paper cup, dip into bubble mixture and blow into the cup.

FAMILY OLYMPICS

- *July Fourth brings many families together. Hold a family olympics using a variety of events to fit all ages. Award medals made using gold-foil-covered chocolate coins attached to ribbon. Add other prizes for extra fun!*

Watermelon Seed Spitting
Give everyone a slice of watermelon and let them practice spitting the seeds as far as they can. When everyone is ready, have a contest and give a prize for the winner. Divide into age groups if needed.

Hula Hoop Contest
Purchase several inexpensive hula hoops from a discount store. Have family members see who can hula hoop the longest. Give awards for the longest, shortest, craziest, etc.

Bubble Blowing Contest
Each participant can chew up to 3 pieces of gum for several minutes. When ready, everyone begins to blow. The person who blows the largest bubble wins! Measuring bubbles is an option.

Shot Put Throw
Blow up medium-sized balloons. Each person gets three chances to throw the inflated balloon as far as possible. Give a prize to the person who throws the longest distance.

Cookie Dash
Divide into two teams. Place a plate with a large cookie on it and a glass of milk a certain distance from each team. Instruct teams to form a line. At the signal, the first person from each team runs to the cookie and eats it. He must not only eat the cookie but must drink the milk before running back. The next person runs down quickly, eats a cookie, and drinks a glass of milk. Each person must take a turn. Have a person at each end pouring glasses of milk and replacing cookies. The first team finished wins.

Pillow Stuff
Have each person place a pillowcase on a pillow and time who can do it fastest. The only catch is that the person must be wearing a pair of boxing gloves.

Find the Flags
Hide numerous small flags (paper flags on toothpicks work great) around the yard. On the signal, have children search for the flags. The child who finds the most flags wins a prize.

Sponge Plunge
Divide into two teams. Place a bucket of water and a large sponge by the first person on each team. Place an empty bucket a certain distance away from each team. At the signal, the first person dips the sponge in water, runs to the other end, and wrings the water into the empty bucket. When the first person runs back, the next person goes. The first team to finish, wins one prize, and the team that is able to squeeze the most water in the bucket, wins another.

Cake Decorating Contest
This is a great contest between families or individuals. Give each family or individual an unfrosted, single layered cake and a bowl of frosting. Give each participant a table knife. Place small bowls filled with candies, fruits, candy sprinkles, chocolate chips, coconut, raisins, nuts, etc. in the center of the table. Set a time limit for decorating. Have pre-appointed judges award prizes when decorating is done. Award prizes for most original, most creative, etc. making sure each cake is awarded a prize. Let everyone eat their masterpiece!

Star Hunt
Cut numerous red, white, and blue stars out of construction paper or cardstock. Die cut stars from a die cut machine also work great. Hide the stars throughout your yard or at a local park. Instruct children to go on a star hunt. Assign different age groups different colors to find if necessary. On the back of certain stars have prizes listed that can be redeemed at the end of the hunt such as sparklers, candy, coins, etc. Children will love it, and the adults will love watching.

Dollar Dive
Fill a child's pool with sand or use the family sand box. Mix numerous coins such as, pennies, nickels, and dimes into the sand. At the signal, let children dive and dig for the coins. The children keep the money they find. Place one quarter in the sand, and the child who finds it wins a dollar bill!

Water Balloon Toss
Fill small balloons with water. Choose partners and stand facing each other. Toss a water filled balloon to the other person. After each toss, the partners must take a step backward. The last set of partners to have an unpopped balloon wins.

Sunshine Scavenger Hunt
Divide into two teams. Each team gets a list of items to collect. Teams go from house to house collecting the items. Only one item per house is allowed. The first team to collect all the items wins! Items to be collected can be Fourth of July and/or summer related. Suggested items are a flag, a star, sparklers, something red, white, or blue, sunglasses, a beach towel, suntan lotion, sunglasses, etc.

Puzzling Puzzles
Purchase 2 puzzles with about 25-50 pieces each. Put puzzles together and spray paint one puzzle blue and the other puzzle red. Stars can be stencilled on with white paint if desired. Let dry and take puzzles apart. When ready to play, divide everyone into two teams. Give each team a puzzle and on the word "GO," the teams put their puzzles together. The first team finished wins.

Seed Counting
Save watermelon seeds during the month of June. Wash and dry. Count the seeds and fill a jar full. At a family reunion or Fourth of July picnic, let each person guess the number of seeds in the jar. Give the winner a watermelon.

Name the President
Gather a variety of coins and paper money. Give prizes for those who can guess the President on each piece of money. Also give a prize to the person who can name the most U.S. Presidents.

HOW WELL DO YOU KNOW OUR COUNTRY?

• *A patriotic quiz!*

Copy the following quiz, and have each family member fill out. Review answers aloud so everyone can learn more about our country. Give a flag as a prize to the person who gets the most answers correct.

PATRIOTIC QUIZ

1. Name the Father of the U.S. Constitution. He was only five foot four inches in height and weighed 97 pounds.

2. Name the three U.S. Presidents who have died on the Fourth of July.

3. Name the only two signers of the U.S. Constitution to become Presidents of the United States.

4. Name the only two signers of the Declaration of Independence to become Presidents of the United States.

5. One of the Founding Fathers was carried in a French Sedan Chair to the Constitutional Convention each day. He was the oldest signer. Name this great patriot.

6. Name the city and state where the signing of the U.S. Constitution and the Declaration of Independence took place.

7. Paul Revere had 16 children and made his famous midnight ride on April 18, 1775. What was the name of his horse?

8. In Abraham Lincoln's *Gettysburg Address* what year did he have in mind when he said, "Four score and seven years ago...?"

9. America is seven letters in length. What were Patrick Henry's seven immortal words?

10. Who is the Author of our National Anthem, *The Star Spangled Banner*?

Patriotic Quiz courtesy of Fred Weeks (Quiz Master)

PATRIOTIC QUIZ ANSWERS
1. James Madison Jr. (Fourth President of the U.S.) **2.** John Adams, Thomas Jefferson, James Monroe **3.** George Washington and James Madison **4.** John Adams and Thomas Jefferson **5.** Benjamin Franklin **6.** Philadelphia, Pennsylvania **7.** Brown Beauty **8.** July 4, 1776 **9.** "Give me liberty or give me death." **10.** Francis Scott Key

HALLOWEEN

MISTER JACK-O'-LANTERN

Old Mister Jack-O'-Lantern you can't frighten me,
    'Cause you're just a pumpkin, as yellow as can be!

I watched my daddy carve you, in fact, I helped him some;
    He took a knife and I a spoon - my but it was fun!

Your eyes are slits, long and thin, your nose is round and wide;
    Your mouth is just a triangle, with crooked teeth inside!

And when we light the candle that stands within your head,
    I like to sit and watch you before I scamper off to bed!

You do look fierce and ugly, but I'm not one bit afraid,
    'Cause you're just a jack-o'-lantern, that my daddy made.

-Author Unknown-

HOLIDAY POPCORN CAKE

• *This cake is great for any holiday! Use different varieties and colors of candies.*

1 c. margarine
1/2 c. light corn syrup
2 c. brown sugar, firmly packed
1 tsp. vanilla
8 qts. popped popcorn
1 1/4 c. M&M brand candies
1 c. nuts (roasted peanuts, almonds, or pecans)
1 c. gumdrops or seasonal candy such as candy corn, etc.

Bring margarine, corn syrup, and sugar to a boil in a heavy saucepan. Boil 1 minute and add vanilla. Pour over popcorn and stir well. Mix in candies and nuts. Press mixture into well greased bundt pan, angel food pan, or 9" x 13" pan. Allow to cool. Invert onto serving plate and slice.

BONES

- *Let these cookies litter your table!*

       4 large egg whites
       1 3/4 c. granulated sugar
       1 tsp. grated orange zest
       1/2 tsp. baking powder
       1 1/2 c. almonds, minced
       1 3/4 c. flour

With an electric mixer beat egg whites, sugar, orange zest, and baking powder until well blended. Add almonds and flour gradually, beating until all ingredients are mixed thoroughly. Cover and place in the refrigerator to chill for at least an hour.

With floured hands, pinch off about 3 tablespoons of dough. On a lightly floured surface, roll dough into an 8" long rope. Fold 1" of each end back onto the dough rope. Pinch ends and shape to look like a bone. Continue until you have made all the dough into bone shapes.

Place bones about 1" apart on a greased and flour-dusted cookie sheet. Bake in a 325 degree oven until cookies are lightly browned on bottoms, about 20 minutes. Remove cookies from oven and transfer to a cooling rack. Makes about 2 dozen cookies.

Note: Bone cookies can be made from a favorite sugar cookie recipe and decorated with white icing. Bread dough can also be shaped into bones to create bone breadsticks.

PUMPKIN PIE AROMA

- *Oooooh......the scent of fresh baked pies will fill the air!*

Score the underside of the lid to your jack-o'-lantern and press in spices such as cinnamon, ginger, and cloves. As the candle burns a wonderful pumpkin pie scent is created.

PUMPKIN SHELL PUNCH BOWL

- *Serve beverages from a hollowed out pumpkin.*

Hollow out a pumpkin by cutting a hole in the top, remove the fiber and seeds, and rinse the inside out well. Draw a jack-o'-lantern face on the pumpkin with markers or paint with acrylic paints. Place the pumpkin in the refrigerator until ready to serve apple cider or your favorite cold drink by pouring it into the pumpkin shell. Add dry ice for a spooky effect if desired. (Be sure to wear gloves when handling dry ice.)

DELICIOUS DEADLY DOUGHNUTS

- *These are to die for!*

1 Tbs. yeast	1 c. mashed potatoes
1/4 c. warm water	1 1/2 tsp. salt
1/2 c. shortening	1/2 tsp. lemon extract
2 c. milk	1/2 tsp. vanilla
1/2 c. granulated sugar	6-8 c. flour
2 large eggs, beaten	

Dissolve yeast in warm water. Set aside. Scald milk with shortening. Add salt, sugar, and enough flour to make a thin batter. Stir in potatoes, eggs, yeast mixture, vanilla, and extract. Add enough flour to make a soft dough.   Let dough rise until doubled.   Roll out dough to 1/2" thickness. Cut dough with a doughnut cutter and let doughnuts rise until double. Deep-fry doughnuts in hot oil (375 degrees), placing raised side into the oil first. Fry until light brown, turning only once. Drain on paper towels. While hot, dip the doughnuts in glaze and drain on a cooling rack placed over a cookie sheet.

Glaze

1 1b. powdered sugar
1/2 tsp. vanilla
1/2 tsp. lemon extract
Hot water

To make glaze, combine powdered sugar, flavorings, and enough hot water to make a thin consistency. Dip hot doughnuts in glaze. Doughnuts can also be dipped into powdered sugar or cinnamon sugar. A chocolate glaze can be made by omitting the lemon extract and adding cocoa powder.

Note: To make quick and easy doughnuts, use refrigerator biscuits. Cut a small circle from the center of each biscuit or press a finger through the center to form a dough ring. Deep-fry in hot oil until golden brown. Dip in glaze or sprinkle with powdered or cinnamon sugar while hot.

LICORICE CARAMELS

- *Soft and chewy, black and gooey.*

1 can (14 oz.) sweetened condensed milk
2 c. granulated sugar
1 c. butter
1/4 tsp. salt
1 1/2 c. light corn syrup
1 tsp. anise extract
Black food coloring

Combine first 5 ingredients in a heavy saucepan and cook until mixture reaches 234 degrees. Stir constantly. Add anise extract and enough black food coloring to obtain desired color. Pour into a buttered 9" x 13" pan and let cool. Cut and wrap in waxed paper. (Other flavors and colors can be added instead of the anise extract and black coloring.)

SPOOKY JUICE FLOAT

- *A green and purple drink.*

Fill a glass half full of grape juice and add a scoop of lime sherbet. Add enough lemon-lime soda to finish filling the glass. Place a candy gummy worm along the rim of the glass to serve.

BLACK BAT BREW

- *The combination of colors in this drink makes it a black beverage.*

1 pkg. grape-flavored unsweetened powdered drink mix
1 pkg. orange-flavored unsweetened powdered drink mix
2 c. granulated sugar
1-2 qts. ginger-ale

Mix well. Serve chilled with Creepy Crawly Ice (see below).

CREEPY CRAWLY ICE

- *This will be sure to get some laughs!*

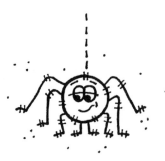

Place a plastic **spider** or **bug** in each individual square of an ice cube tray. Fill with water and freeze. Serve as you would ice in your favorite Halloween beverage.

Freeze a rubber or plastic **snake** in a gelatin mold filled with water. What a fun surprise your guests will have when they find a snake in the ice ring floating in the punch bowl.

PUMPKIN BOWLS

- *Serve hot, hearty stew from these pumpkin-shaped bread bowls.*

1 loaf frozen bread dough, thawed
1 Tbs. water
1 egg, beaten

Cut approximately 1" off the end of the loaf of dough. Cut into 4 equal parts and shape into stems. Cover and place in refrigerator until ready for use. Divide remaining part of the loaf into 4 equal parts and roll into smooth balls. Place on a greased cookie sheet, cover, and let rise until doubled. Make a slit in the top of each bread ball and gently insert a dough stem. Combine egg and water and brush over the dough. Bake at 350 degrees for 20-25 minutes or until golden brown. Let cool. Slice off the top of each bowl and hollow out the soft interior. Fill with soup, stew, or chili. Makes 4 bread bowls.

SPIDER SUCKERS

- *A creative treat. Great idea for room mothers.*

For **each** spider you will need:

1 round lollipop with orange wrapping
    (Tootsie Roll brand Pops)
1 black pom-pom (1")
2 large, black chenille stems
2 wiggly craft eyes (5mm)
Hot glue
1/8 yard (1/8" wide) purple ribbon (opt.)

To assemble: *(see illustration)*

1. Glue pom-pom to lollipop as shown below. *(Figure 1)*
2. Cut chenille stems to 6" in length. You should have 4 pieces total.
3. Lay 3 chenille stems side by side and twist the 4th around so you have a bundle. *(Figure 2)*
4. Separate chenille stems apart to form "legs" and bend up the tips of each to make "feet."
5. Glue the bundle of "legs" to the center of the lollipop opposite to where the pom-pom is glued. *(Figure 3)*
6. Glue two eyes on the pom-pom.
7. Tie a bow from the ribbon and glue to top of pom-pom or "chin" of spider depending on if you want a male or female.

Note: You may wish to use smaller chenille stems in orange and black. Twist together to make striped legs. Three 6" pieces of chenille may also be used which creates 6 total legs and looks just as good as the 8 legs.

Figure 1

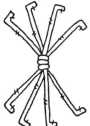

Figure 2

Figure 3

CHOCOLATE TARANTULAS

- *Eat these quick before they creep away!*

1 c. semi-sweet chocolate chips
1 c. butterscotch chips
3/4 c. salted peanuts
1 1/2 c. chow mein noodles
Small candies (opt.)

In a double boiler, over low heat, combine the chocolate and butterscotch chips. Stir until smooth. Remove from heat and stir in peanuts and noodles. Drop by spoonfuls onto waxed paper and let cool. Add two small candy "eyes" if desired.

FISHING FOR TREATS

- *A fun way to distribute treats on Halloween night.*

Open your front door. Attach a dark blanket, piece of butcher paper, or cardboard, across the open space securing it to both sides of the door frame. Be sure to leave an open space above the blanket. Make a "fishing pole" from a broom or dowel and attach a string with a wooden clothespin on the end. Have someone sit by your front door (dressed up scary, of course) who can help you when the trick-or-treaters come. Let each child throw the string and clothespin over the blanket to "fish." Attach wrapped candy, plastic Halloween novelties, small toys, or gift certificates to the clothespin. Make sure to have scary music playing and make cackling sounds when each child "sends over their line!"

TRICK-OR-TREATS

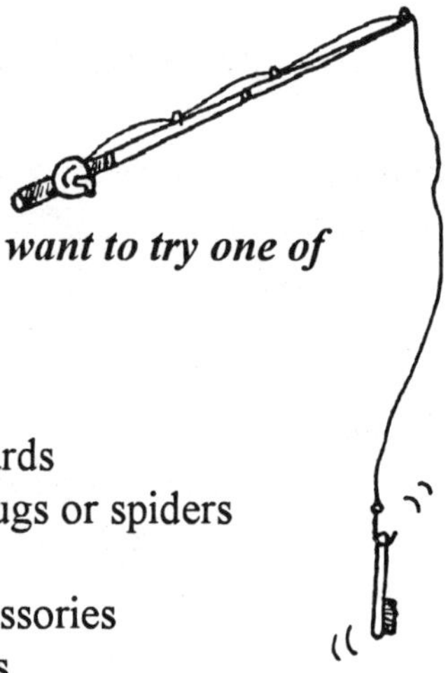

- *Children often enjoy items other than candy for Halloween. You may want to try one of the following items this year:*

coins	gift certificates	stickers
small books	book markers	sports cards
combs	crayons	plastic bugs or spiders
toy rings	toothbrushes	pencils
balloons	whistles	hair accessories
plastic trinkets	bubbles	shoelaces

HALLOWEEN FACE PAINT

- *A safe alternative to masks.*

1 tsp. cornstarch
1/2 tsp. cold cream
1/2 tsp. water

Blend ingredients well. Add food coloring one drop at a time until you reach the desired color. Paint on face with a small paintbrush or cotton swab. Remove with soap and water.

For a **brown** color face paint, add 1 teaspoon white shortening to 2 teaspoons cocoa.

> To keep your children visible on Halloween night have them wear a reflector. Using a permanent black marker draw a pumpkin face on a round orange reflector and attach to clothing.

NEIGHBORHOOD PUMPKIN WALK

- *Make this pumpkin walk an annual Halloween event.*

Pass flyers around your neighborhood announcing a "neighborhood pumpkin walk." Include date and time (best if done before Halloween night and right after dusk). Instruct everyone to carve or decorate one or more pumpkins and set out on their porch or driveway at a certain time. Neighbors can then walk around to see all the fun creations. If desired, awards could be presented and refreshments served. This is a great way to get acquainted with your neighbors.

PUMPKIN LUMINARIA

- *Light up your driveway and sidewalk.*

You will need 6 (or more if desired) pumpkins close to the same size. Cut the tops off and remove the seeds. Using an apple corer or a drill, make holes through the sides of the pumpkins about 2" apart. Cover the entire pumpkin with holes. Small triangle shapes can be cut in the pumpkins instead of round holes if desired. Set along driveway and put small candles inside each pumpkin. Light at dusk and enjoy! These also make great centerpieces.

JACK-O'-LANTERN CARVING

- *Carve pumpkins from the bottom up.*

A unique way to carve a jack-o'-lantern is to cut a round hole in the bottom of the pumpkin instead of the top. Discard the bottom piece. This prevents the lid from shrinking, falling in and snuffing the candle out. Place the candle on a plate or pie tin and light it. Set the pumpkin over the top of the burning candle.

PUMPKIN TOTEM POLE

- *Make a tall statement!*

Pound a piece of metal conduit pipe or metal post into the ground. (Length of pipe needed depends on size and number of pumpkins used.) Carve 5-7 pumpkins in graduating size. Make sure to carve some of the facial features large enough to reach through to light the candles. Place several small votive candles in each pumpkin **before** stacking. Puncture the bottom of each pumpkin. Place each pumpkin over the pole starting with the largest. Use some of the pieces carved from the pumpkins to make ears, noses, etc. You may need to trim the tops of each pumpkin so the next one will sit straight on top of it. Light the candles with long matches.

CHOCOLATE SPIDERS AND WEBS

- *Delicious as a candy or served on top of a Halloween dessert.*

Melt 1 c. semi-sweet chocolate chips and 1 teaspoon of shortening over low heat in a double boiler (or in a microwave on medium heat, stirring every 30 seconds). Remove from heat and cool for about 10 minutes. Place chocolate in pastry bag with a small round tip.

Spiders   Place waxed paper on a cookie sheet. Squeeze two small circles of chocolate to form a body and head (see illustration). Squeeze 4 legs coming out on each side of the body.

Webs   Trace pattern (below) onto plain paper. Put pattern on a cookie sheet under waxed paper. Squeeze chocolate following the lines of the pattern.

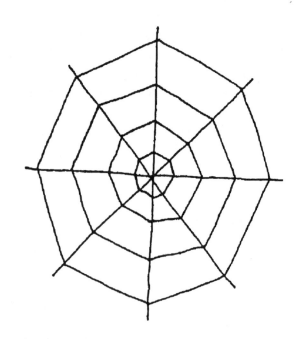

If chocolate is too runny to hold its shape, let it cool for several minutes. Chill the webs and spiders in the freezer for a few minutes until set. Gently peel the waxed paper away from the chocolate. The spider webs are very delicate, so handle carefully. Add two tiny white icing eyes on spider if desired. These spiders and webs can be stored in a single layer, separated by waxed paper for up to a month in the freezer. Makes about 1 dozen spider webs or 2 dozen spiders.

SCARY SNACK FACES

- *A creative sandwich decorating contest for children.*

This can be a fun game as well as a snack for children. Give each child two pieces of bread and have him/her spread each one with peanut butter. Have several bowls filled with things such as candy corn, raisins, dried bananas, nuts, chocolate chips, miniature marshmallows, licorice strings, cereals, etc. Set a timer for 3 to 5 minutes, depending on the age group. Let the children decorate their bread with a scary face using the items in the bowls. When finished, have everyone vote on the face that is the scariest, funniest, happiest, silliest, spookiest, etc. Let the children eat their finished product.

DRACULA TEETH

- *A delicious bite!*

Slice two green apples into 1/2" wedges. Spread one side of each with peanut butter or marshmallow creme. With peanut butter sides facing each other, place five candy corns pointed ends down between the apple wedges. The green skin should look like lips and the candy like teeth.

FRANKIE COOKIES

- *These cookies are ghastly green!*

Purchase square or rectangle creme filled cookies. Gently pull apart cookies and press the creme filled side into green colored sugar to coat. Use the non-creme side for another use. Place chocolate icing in a pastry bag with a small round tip or in a plastic bag with the corner snipped. Squeeze on a crooked mouth, and a jagged hair line. Pipe on two white eyes with vanilla icing and place on a dot of chocolate to make pupils in the eyes. Add a small round candy on each side of the bottom of the cookie to add the finishing Frankenstein touch!

WITCH HAT COOKIES

- *Small witch hat cookies are perfect for snacking.*

Use icing to attach an unwrapped chocolate kiss or the pointed end of an ice cream cone, to the center of a round fudge-striped shortbread cookie. You now have a pointed witch hat. Using a pastry tube with a small round tip, pipe on an icing bow with orange frosting.

PEANUTTY GHOSTS

- *These ghostly cookies will disappear in no time.*

You will need to purchase peanut-shaped sandwich cookies. Melt some vanilla flavored almond bark in a double boiler over low heat. Dip each cookie approximately 2/3 of the way into the melted almond bark. Add two tiny chocolate chips or small candies for eyes. Place on waxed paper to cool.

VAMPIRE CHILI CUPS

- *Great for a cold spooky night.*

    1-2 small cans of chili
    1/3 c. grated cheddar cheese
    1 pkg. refrigerator biscuits
    1/3 c. chopped onion (optional)

Place one biscuit in each cup of a muffin tin that has been sprayed with cooking spray. Flatten and spread biscuit to fit the muffin cups. Fill each biscuit 2/3 full with chili and sprinkle with grated cheese and chopped onion. Bake at 350 degrees for 20-25 minutes. Makes 10 chili cups.

CINNAMON POPCORN GHOSTS

- *Kids love these edible ghosts.*

    4 qts. popped popcorn
    1/4 tsp. cinnamon
    6 c. miniature marshmallows
    1/4 c. margarine or butter

Melt marshmallows and margarine over low heat, stirring constantly. Add cinnamon. Pour over popcorn and toss to coat. Shape into ghosts and add small candy for eyes. Insert a wooden skewer or wooden stick to eat as a lollipop.

SQUIGGLY SQUEEZE BOTTLE NOODLES

- *Creative noodles to add to soup.*

    1 egg, beaten
    1/2 tsp. salt
    1/2 c. milk
    1 c. flour

Mix ingredients together and pour into a squeeze bottle (such as an empty ketchup bottle). For each noodle, squeeze a small amount into the boiling water of your favorite soup. Cook 10 minutes.

CREEPY ORANGE SHELL GELATIN

- *Treats with a surprise inside!*

Wash oranges. Cut in half and scoop out the pulp. Mix orange gelatin, following directions and pour into half orange shells. Set orange halves in muffin cups to keep level and refrigerate until firm. To add a creepy touch to the gelatin, press gummy worms or spiders into the gelatin when it is partially set. Serve with or without whipped topping. If necessary, cut a thin slice off the bottom of the orange so it will remain level when serving.

EASY CARAMEL POPCORN

- *A quick and delicious popcorn.*

    5-6 qts. popped popcorn
    1/2 c. margarine
    1/2 c. light corn syrup
    2 1/4 c. brown sugar

Place margarine, syrup, and sugar in a saucepan. Place over medium-high heat and bring to a boil. Stir until sugar is dissolved, the margarine is melted, and all the ingredients are blended well. Boil 1 minute. Remove from heat and pour over the popped corn.

PUMPKIN FACE POPCORN BALLS

- *A delightful treat or gift. This is a fun project for children to help with.*

5-6 qts. popped popcorn	1/2 c. light corn syrup
3 c. miniature marshmallows	1 1/2 tsp. vanilla
1 c. margarine	Orange food coloring
1 1/4 c. granulated sugar	Candy corn, jelly beans,
	or other small candies

In a large mixing bowl, mix together popped popcorn and marshmallows. Set aside. Melt margarine in a heavy saucepan and add sugar and corn syrup. Bring to boil over medium heat. Boil for three minutes, stirring constantly. Remove from heat and stir in vanilla and orange food coloring. Pour hot syrup over popcorn and marshmallow mixture and mix to coat. When mixture is cool enough to handle, shape into balls and add a face if desired. To make a face on the popcorn ball, use candy corn, jelly beans, or other small candies. Wrap in plastic wrap or cellophane and tie with raffia, jute, or a Halloween ribbon.

WORMY BAKED APPLES

- *These apples have a delicious filling and a worm is an added bonus!*

6 large Golden Delicious apples	1/4 c. margarine
1/2 c. chopped nuts	1/2 tsp. cinnamon
1/2 c. raisins	1/2 tsp. nutmeg
1/2 c. brown sugar	6 gummy worms
1/4 c. water	1 c. whipping cream (opt.)

Wash and core apples from the blossom end, making sure you don't core all the way through the stem end. Mix nuts and raisins together and fill cored apple with mixture. Set filled apples in a baking dish. In a sauce pan, mix the brown sugar, water, margarine, cinnamon, and nutmeg. Stir over high heat until mixture boils. Pour hot syrup around apples. Bake uncovered at 350 degrees, 30-35 minutes. Baste the apples occasionally with syrup, until apples are tender when pierced and skin begins to crack. When apples are done, remove from oven and cool for at least 10 minutes. Serve each apple in a small bowl and spoon syrup around it. In the top of each apple, cut a hole large enough for one of the gummy worms and tuck one end into each apple, leaving most of the worm hanging out. Pour cream over apples if desired. Makes 6 wormy servings.

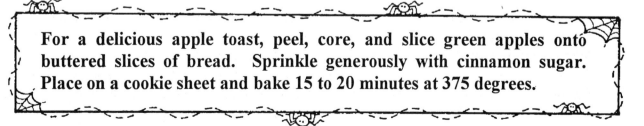

For a delicious apple toast, peel, core, and slice green apples onto buttered slices of bread. Sprinkle generously with cinnamon sugar. Place on a cookie sheet and bake 15 to 20 minutes at 375 degrees.

MUDDY WORM PIE

- *One bite of this worm pie and you will be hooked!*

Crust   20 creme filled chocolate sandwich cookies
5 Tbs. margarine, melted

Place cookies in a plastic bag and crush with a rolling pin. Pour crushed cookies into a mixing bowl and stir in the melted margarine. Mix well. Pour mixture into a 9" pie plate and press with the back of a spoon to form a shell. Place in the freezer for 15 minutes.

Filling   1 qt. ice cream, chocolate or vanilla
10-15 gummy worms
Chocolate sauce
Whipped topping

Soften ice cream and pour into a large mixing bowl. Stir the gummy worms into the ice cream and pour into the chilled pie shell. Add a layer of chocolate sauce. When ready to serve, top with whipped topping. To be creative, color the whipped topping orange by adding a small amount of food coloring. Keep this dessert a surprise. It is fun to watch someone's face as they bite into those tasty, gooey, yummy, gummy worms.

HOBGOBLIN ORANGE DELIGHT

- *A smooth and creamy dessert or salad.*

2 small pkgs. (3 oz. each) vanilla pudding mix (cooked type)
2 small pkgs. (3 oz. each) orange gelatin
1 container (8 oz.) whipped topping
2 cans (10 oz. each) mandarin oranges, drained

Cook pudding according to package directions, except use water instead of milk. While hot, stir in the gelatin. Chill overnight to set. When set, add whipped topping and mix well. Stir in mandarin oranges. Place in refrigerator to reset.

UNEARTHLY PEANUT BUTTER APPLES

- *Out of this world!*

8 medium-sized apples
2 c. peanut butter chips
3 Tbs. vegetable oil
8 wooden sticks
Chopped nuts, crushed cereal, or coconut

Wash and dry apples. Remove stems and insert a wooden stick in the top of each. Melt peanut butter chips with oil over low heat, stirring constantly until smooth. Remove from heat and dip each apple in the mixture. Roll in nuts, cereal, or coconut. Refrigerate on waxed paper to cool.

BEWITCHING PUMPKIN CUPCAKES

- *These cupcakes won't last long!*

1 yellow cake mix	1/2 tsp. nutmeg
3/4 c. water	1 tsp. cinnamon
2 eggs	1/8 tsp. cloves
1 c. plain canned pumpkin	1/4 tsp. soda
1/2 tsp. ginger	2 tsp. grated orange zest

Place all ingredients in a mixing bowl and blend well. Place cupcake liners in muffin tins and fill 2/3 full with batter. Bake at 375 degrees for 18-20 minutes or until a toothpick inserted comes out clean. Remove from oven and cool on wire rack. Frost with Howling Good Licorice Frosting below.

HOWLING GOOD LICORICE FROSTING

- *Unique!*

1/2 c. margarine, softened
3 c. powdered sugar
2 Tbs. milk
1 tsp. anise extract

In small bowl, cream together margarine and sugar. Add milk and extract and beat until smooth. Add black food coloring if desired.

WICKEDLY DELICIOUS TOPPING

- *Marvelous on pumpkin cakes.*

1 pt. whipping cream, whipped
3/4 c. brown sugar

Whip cream until spreading consistency and stir in brown sugar. Makes enough topping for a two-layer cake or 24 cupcakes.

JACK-O'-LANTERN COOKIES

- *This jack-o'-lantern cookie has stained glass features.*

1/2 c. butter or margarine	2 tsp. baking powder
1 c. granulated sugar	1/4 tsp. salt
1 egg	1 Tbs. milk
1 tsp. vanilla	Orange and green food coloring
2 c. flour	Hard candies (lemon drops), crushed

Cream together butter and sugar. Add egg and vanilla. Beat in flour, baking powder, and salt. Add milk if batter is too stiff. Color 1/8 of the dough green and the remaining dough orange. Roll out orange dough and cut with a round cookie cutter to make pumpkin shapes. Place on foil covered cookie sheet. Roll and shape stems out of the green dough and attach to top of each pumpkin. Carefully cut out spaces for the eyes, nose, and mouth with a knife. Fill holes with a small amount of crushed hard candies. (Too much candy will run and stick to the bottom.) Bake at 350 degrees for 8-10 minutes. Do not allow to brown. Cool for about 10 minutes, then carefully peel off foil.

JACK-O'-LANTERN SANDWICH

- *Great served with salad and chili.*

Slices of dark rye or pumpernickel bread
Grated parmesan cheese
Jack-o'-lantern paper face pattern (below)

Trace the pattern below onto a piece of paper or design a jack-o'-lantern face of your own. Cut the face pieces out and arrange the paper pieces onto a slice of dark bread. With the pattern in place generously sprinkle parmesan cheese over the top of the pattern and bread. Remove the pattern carefully to reveal the face, and place the bread on a cookie sheet. Place under the broiler until cheese is slightly brown and bread is toasted.

FESTIVE FRUIT FACE

- *Decorate orange bottled fruit.*

From black construction paper, felt, or contact paper, cut triangle eyes, nose, and a toothy grin. Use pattern (at left) for the jack-o'-lantern face or design your own. Glue across the front of a jar of orange colored fruit or jam, such as peaches or apricots. With pinking shears, cut a circle of green fabric, approximately 9" in diameter and place over the jar lid. Tie with raffia, jute, or ribbon and attach a small decorated card for gift giving.

HALLOWEEN PANCAKES

- *A fun family breakfast that adds a flavor of the season.*

Mix enough pancake batter to serve your family. From a cup, drizzle the batter onto the hot griddle in the form of a ghost or a pumpkin. You can add some mashed pumpkin or orange food coloring to the batter if desired. Place a bowl of raisins and chocolate chips on the table so everyone can add eyes to their ghosts and a face to their pumpkins.

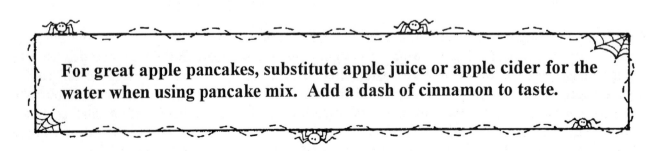

For great apple pancakes, substitute apple juice or apple cider for the water when using pancake mix. Add a dash of cinnamon to taste.

HOLIDAY BAG TOPPERS

- *Creatively top a bag filled with goodies. A great idea for room mothers.*

Cut a 7 1/2" x 5" piece of white or colored cardstock. Fold length-wise down the center. Decorate with clip art, stickers, rubber stamps, writing, poems, etc. Cut bottom edge with decorative paper scissors. Staple to the top of a quart or snack-size zip top plastic bag filled with candy or treats.

GOBLIN HANDS

- *A haunting hand treat.*

Use a **clear** plastic glove. (A great place to get these is from your local bakery or deli. **Don't** use rubber or latex medical gloves.) In the tip of each finger place a candy corn or black jelly bean. This makes the fingernails. Fill glove with plain, popped popcorn. Place a plastic spider ring on one of the fingers to add the final spooky touch. Secure the top with an elastic or baggie tie. Add a cute Halloween bow around the top.

LOLLIPOP PUMPKIN HEAD

- *This pumpkin has a head full of colorful lollipops!*

Wash and dry a large pumpkin. Draw a jack-o'-lantern face on the pumpkin using a marker or acrylic paint. Using a metal skewer or nail, make holes randomly over the top of the pumpkin. Insert a colorful lollipop in each hole.   This is a great idea for room mothers to display class treats or a cute way to dispense candy to trick-or-treaters.

PUMPKIN TREAT CANS

- *Paint empty soup cans to create fun treat containers.*

Wash and thoroughly dry empty soup or vegetable cans. Place a block of wood inside the can to stabilize it while you pound a nail through the can 1/2" below the rim. Remove the nail to make holes for the handle to attach. Remove the block, place the can on newspaper, and spray the outside of the can with orange spray paint. Spray with several coats allowing each to dry well (you can also use orange acrylic paint instead of the spray paint).   Stencil a jack-o'-lantern face on one side of the can using black paint or a permanent marker. Attach a wire handle and a raffia bow to the side of the handle. Fill with treats and wrap in cellophane if desired.

To make a ghost, paint can white with black eyes. Be creative. Try painting a can to look like a witch, Frankenstein, etc. Buttons or glitter can be glued on the cans. The possibilities are endless, and this makes a great, inexpensive project for school or friends.

A SPOOKY TALE

- *Dim the lights and enjoy the tale! A game to be played with a group.*

Gather at least 20 items in a big paper sack. Have everyone sit in a circle.   Have the host or hostess start the "spooky tale" with one of the story starter suggestions or create your own. The next person in the circle must pull an item out of the sack and add several lines to the story which must include the item they picked from the sack. Continue around the circle with each person picking an item from the sack and adding lines to the story. Continue until all the items are gone. This game will create a fun story that will bring lots of laughs!

Story starters:

Last night I heard a noise in my cellar...

I was at the graveyard when the moon was full...

A long time ago on a faraway planet...

Deep in the dark, lonely forest...

No one had seen Mr. R. U. Bones for many years until one day...

Suggested items for sack:

paintbrush	comb	ruler	watch
pan	fork	hammer	measuring cup
sock	elastic	pencil	cotton balls
book	stick	rock	small pumpkin
nail	banana	hat	plastic spider
candy bar	coin	rope	toy snake
plastic fangs	mirror	candle	adhesive bandage
flashlight	whistle	bell	plastic eye

Any small item or Halloween novelty would work great.

NEWSPAPER CEILING

- *An inexpensive decorating idea.*

To make a nice spooky atmosphere at a party try this.   String wires across the entire room approximately 2 feet apart. Holding a newspaper horizontally with the fold up, cut slits 2" apart across the entire newspaper, cutting until 2" from the fold. Slip the newspapers end to end with the folds over the wires. The slits will be hanging down. This will create a low ceiling effect with very minimal cost.

SPIDER TOSS

- *Great game for a carnival or a children's party.*

Cover a large, square piece of plywood with heavy black fabric or paint it black. Staple the **hook** side of white Velcro brand hook and loop tape in the shape of a large web onto the plywood. Save the loop side for another project. (This will use quite a bit of Velcro, depending on web size, so watch for sales.)

To make beanbag spiders, sew small round or square pieces of heavy duty black fabric together and fill with dry beans. Stitch or glue several pieces of the **loop** side of black Velcro on both sides of the beanbag. Legs can be made by sewing pieces of the black Velcro to the sides of the beanbag. Add two white beads for eyes if desired.

To play: Have each child stand and throw the spiders to the center of the web. The spiders will stick to the web. Give a prize to the child who gets the most spiders in the center of the web.

HALLOWEEN BEANBAGS

- *Homemade beanbags bring hours of fun.*

Cut two 6" x 6" squares from a Halloween print fabric. With wrong sides together, sew around sides (1/4" seam allowance) leaving a small opening to turn. Turn and fill beanbag 2/3 full with pinto, red, or white beans. Sew opening closed.

Beanbags can be made in any shape or size from any fabric. They are inexpensive and quick to make. A child would love a stack of colorful beanbags for any holiday or for everyday fun. Use up your scraps of fabric and make beanbags for all the trick-or-treaters.

PUMPKIN CARVING CONTEST

- *A fun activity for an adult Halloween party.*

Cover a long table with newspaper. Give each couple or small group a pumpkin and knife. Tell them you will give them 30 minutes to carve their pumpkins before they will be judged. The only stipulation is they must decorate their pumpkin with all the items in a sack you give them. Have each sack contain different items such as nails, yarn, nuts, spools, ribbon, plastic sunglasses, old batteries, carrots, wigs, straws, toothpicks, hats, etc. Be creative! Present a fun award for **each** pumpkin such as the most creative, spookiest, silliest, ugliest, etc. Let your guests take their pumpkins home.

HOWL-OWEEN TABLE SETTING

- *Creative table decorations.*

Sweet Napkin Rings
Carefully thread black and orange jelly beans, gumdrops, or candy corn using a sharp needle and strong thread. Make desired length and tie together ends to form a circle. Use as a napkin ring.

Cobweb Table
Set a Halloween table ready for dinner guests or your family. Drape table with purchased spider webbing, making the table look as if it is covered in cobwebs. Be sure to cover plates, centerpieces, etc. Add some plastic spiders for a creepy touch.

Double Sided Jack-O'-Lantern
Carve a pumpkin with two faces. Carve one face on one side and a different face on the other. Use for a centerpiece on a table and guests on either side will enjoy the faces.

Paper Sack Pumpkin
Fill a paper sack with crumpled newspaper and tie at the top to make a pumpkin shape. Paint or spray with orange paint. Paint the stem part green (top of sack) and add a raffia bow and autumn leaves.

Pumpkin Face Favors
Use miniature pumpkins or oranges for jack-o'-lantern favors. When using oranges, place short pieces of green or brown pipe cleaners in the tops to make stems. Paint the jack-o'-lantern features with a black felt-tipped marker. Place in center of table or use at each place setting.

A BOO-TIFUL GIFT

- *A rose container filled with cookies.*

Do you need a quick gift? Fill a plastic long-stemmed rose container (available at a florist) with creme filled cookies. These containers are the perfect size for many cookies to fit in a row, single file. Try orange-filled chocolate sandwich cookies available in October and add a colorful bow. Wrap with stretchy, spider webbing. Great for teachers, neighbors, or your favorite person.

SPIDER SPUN PLATES

- *Serve a Halloween dessert on these icing webs.*

Place black or white icing in a pastry bag with a small round tip. Pipe an icing web onto a round paper or serving plate, covering most of the plate. Serve ice cream, cake, etc. on web. Top dessert with a spider made with a creme filled cookie with thin licorice legs and icing eyes.

WICKED WITCH CARD GAME

- *A Halloween twist on the children's card game Old Maid.*

Cut 41 cards from orange cardstock measuring 4" x 3". You will need to find a sticker or picture of a wicked looking witch and glue to one of the cards. You will also need to purchase 2 each of 20 different Halloween stickers so you have 20 pairs. Stick one on each of the orange cards. You now have a set of 41 playing cards. Laminate for durability, if desired.

This game is played like Old Maid with the wicked witch being the "old maid." The object is to play and make pairs with your cards without being stuck with the wicked witch.

To play:

1. Shuffle the cards and deal them to the players (3 or more players). It will not matter if some players have more cards than other players do.
2. Have each player look for pairs in his/her hand and discard the pairs.
3. When it is your turn, draw a card from the person on your left. If you have a card that matches the one you drew then discard the pair. If you do not have a match, add the card to your hand and the play moves to the next person on your left.
4. Whoever has the "wicked witch" after all the cards have been played is the unluky one!

ROASTED PUMPKIN SEEDS

- *A crispy, nutty, fall snack.*

Wash pumpkin seeds and pat dry with a paper towel. Toss seeds with 1 tablespoon of melted butter per cup of seeds. Sprinkle lightly with salt and spread in a single layer on a cookie sheet. Bake in a 250 degree oven until seeds are crisp and brown. This is usually 1 to 1 1/2 hours. Shake or stir a few times for even browning. Serve warm or store in refrigerator.

COOKIE CUTTER CREATURES

- *Mini Halloween shapes add "life" to your meals.*

Make your favorite green or pasta salad. With miniature cookie cutters, cut ghosts, moons, pumpkins, bats, etc. out of cheese or ham slices. Toss into salad or use as a garnish.

Another idea using miniature Halloween cookie cutters is to cut shapes from bread. Butter bread shapes and place under broiler until butter melts. Remove and sprinkle with cinnamon sugar.

HALLOWEEN ACTIVITIES

• *Need some party games?*

Musical Tombstones
Make cardboard tombstones of desired size and decorate. Place tombstones randomly on the floor around the room making sure there is one less than the number of players. Play as you would musical chairs having each child stand, sit, or lay on the tombstone when the music stops. Remove a tombstone and eliminate the person without a tombstone each round. The one person remaining at the end wins. Spooky music (available at discount stores, the local library, or create your own) adds a perfect touch!

Pin-Ups
Play pin the wart on the witches nose, pin the face on the pumpkin, or pin the tail on the black cat.

Creative Mask Contest
Have supplies available to make fun masks (paper plates, scissors, paper bags, glitter, glue, crepe paper, feathers, jewels, markers, crayons, etc.), and let each person create! Have a contest for the scariest, funniest, most creative, etc. and make sure each person gets an award.

Lights Out Game
Give each person a blank piece of paper and a pencil. Turn the lights out so it is totally dark. Instruct everyone to draw a jack-o'-lantern on their piece of paper. After several minutes turn on the lights and give a prize for the best, silliest, scariest, etc.

String-Ups
Tie a string or piece of yarn to an apple stem, doughnut, or cookie and suspend it from the ceiling or doorway. Have two children at a time race to eat the treat. No hands allowed. When they have finished, tie treats up for the next two children.

Giggling Game
Everyone sits in a circle on the floor. Someone starts the game by throwing a handkerchief into the air. While the handkerchief is in the air everyone laughs out loud. As soon as the handkerchief hits the floor the laughing must stop immediately. The first person to make a sound becomes "it" and he/she then throws the handkerchief into the air. Great fun!

Halloween Word Game
Write words relating to Halloween on small pieces of paper. Use such words as witch, pumpkin, boo, spook, bat, cat, ghost, vampire, jack-o'-lantern, etc. Fold and pass one or two to each player. The players sit in a circle and one person who is "it" will point to someone and ask them a question about any subject. The player then has to answer the question using their word in the answer. If the person who is "it" guesses the right word, the two players exchange places. Let everyone have a turn.

Spider Web Game
Cut long pieces of yarn or string into equal lengths. Cut a piece for each person playing the game. Start each piece of string in a common place and weave throughout a room. Wrap string around and under furniture and entangle it on chair legs and other pieces of string. Players are assigned one piece of string. At the word "GO," each player starts to wind their string into a ball, untangling the "web" as they go. The first person to reach the end of their string, wins a prize. Have small favors or treats tied to the end of each string. This game can also be played outside.

Thanksgiving

BLESSING MIX

- *Each ingredient in this snack mix symbolizes something associated with Thanksgiving.*

  2 c. Bugles brand corn snacks (shaped as a cornucopia, a horn of plenty)
  2 c. pretzels (represent arms folded in thanks and prayer)
  1 c. candy corn (during the first winter, the pilgrims were each allotted only 5
        kernels of corn per day because food was so scarce)
  1 c. dried or candy fruits (Thanksgiving is the celebration of the harvest)
  1 c. peanuts or sunflower seeds (seeds represent the potential of a
        bounteous harvest for the next season if they are planted and well tended)

In a large bowl mix all ingredients together. Other ingredients such as dry cereals, candies, or marshmallows can also be added. Make this mix as a family and eat while discussing each ingredient and how it relates to Thanksgiving.

THANKSGIVING DAY JOURNAL

- *Thinking about a new tradition? A family journal will last a lifetime.*

On Thanksgiving Day, record in a special book the names of guests, what was served, and any other important tidbits about the day. Have each person present write a short message in the book. Each year you will enjoy reading the messages of thanks and enjoy the memories of holidays past.

THANK YOU LETTER

- *Write a letter of thanks.*

Why not take the time this holiday season and write a letter to someone who has been an influence in your life? A thank you letter or note of appreciation can be a gift treasured for a lifetime. This would be a great family tradition to start.

PUMPKIN NOG

- *A delicious holiday beverage, perfect for Thanksgiving.*

1 qt. vanilla ice cream, softened
1 qt. milk
1 can (30 oz.) pumpkin pie mix
Nutmeg to taste

In a large bowl, stir ice cream until smooth. Add milk and pumpkin pie mix (mix includes spices). Cover and chill until ready to serve. Just before serving, stir again and sprinkle with nutmeg.

BAKED CORNUCOPIA

- *A great holiday centerpiece. Fill with cheeses, fruits, rolls, nuts, or greenery.*

2 lbs. frozen or homemade bread dough
1 egg white
Disposable round aluminum foil pizza pan
Non-stick cooking spray

Use the foil pizza pan to make a form to bake the cornucopia on. Roll the pan into a cone shape with the opening about 6" in diameter. Curve the small end to resemble a horn shape. Spray the outside of the aluminum cone with the non-stick cooking spray and place on a greased cookie sheet.

If using frozen bread dough, let thaw. Roll dough into a large rectangle, 1/4" thick. Cut the dough into 1 1/2" wide strips. You will need approximately 10 strips. Starting at the tapered end, wrap strips of dough around cone. Overlap strips about 1/2" as you wrap. When adding new strips, pinch ends together making sure to join them on the bottom of the cornucopia. Keep adding strips and wrapping dough around the cone until the entire cone is covered.

To make a decorative edge along the opening, roll two ropes of dough approximately 12" in length. Twist ropes together and place along the edge of the last dough strip on the cornucopia. Gently press together. Brush dough with beaten egg white and let rise for 20 minutes. Bake at 350 degrees for 25 minutes. Cover cornucopia loosely with foil to prevent over-browning and bake for 25 more minutes or until bread sounds hollow when tapped. Cool 15 minutes. Gently compress and remove aluminum cone.

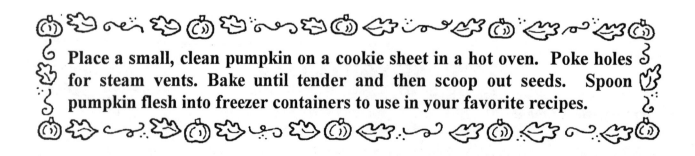

Place a small, clean pumpkin on a cookie sheet in a hot oven. Poke holes for steam vents. Bake until tender and then scoop out seeds. Spoon pumpkin flesh into freezer containers to use in your favorite recipes.

INDIAN CORN ON A STICK

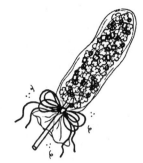

- *Keep a supply of these popcorn treats on hand for all your little snackers!*

    3/4 c. margarine
    60 large marshmallows
    3 qts. popped popcorn
    1/4 c. peanuts (or any other coarsely chopped nuts)
    1/4 c. shredded coconut
    1 c. chopped dried fruits (cranberries, apricots,
              pineapple, apples, or raisins)

Melt margarine and marshmallows over low heat. Pour over popped corn and stir in nuts, coconut, and dried fruits. When cool enough to handle, mold popcorn mixture into ear of corn shapes approximately 6" long. Insert a wooden stick, wooden skewer, or dowel in the end of each. Place on a greased cookie sheet or waxed paper to set. Makes approximately 20-25 "Indian corn" servings. Wrap with cellophane and tie with a raffia bow.

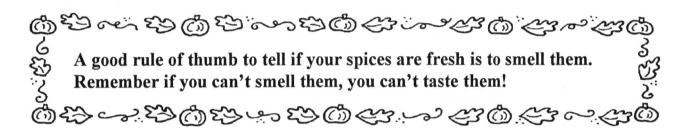

A good rule of thumb to tell if your spices are fresh is to smell them. Remember if you can't smell them, you can't taste them!

CANDIED CRANBERRIES

- *A great garnish for a holiday ham or Thanksgiving yams.*

Spread 3 cups fresh cranberries in a glass baking dish. Sprinkle with 1 1/2 c. granulated sugar. Cover dish tightly with a lid or foil. Bake at 375 degrees for approximately 1 hour (or microwave on high for 4-5 minutes). Stir occasionally during baking time. Cranberries will become soft and have a sweet glaze on them. Yum!

CANDY CORN BRITTLE

- *Instead of peanuts, use candy corn.*

Make your favorite peanut brittle recipe. Instead of stirring in peanuts, stir in 1 cup candy corn. Pour onto a greased cookie sheet and pull candy thin with spoons. Let cool and break apart.

PUMPKIN FREEZE

- *A melt-in-your-mouth pumpkin dessert.*

Crust

2 c. crushed gingersnap cookies
1/3 c. butter or margarine, melted
2 Tbs. brown sugar

Mix all ingredients together and firmly press into a 9" x 13" baking dish. Chill.

Filling

1 1/2 c. plain canned pumpkin
1/2 c. brown sugar
1/2 tsp. cinnamon
1/2 tsp. ginger
1/4 tsp. cloves
1/8 tsp. salt
1 qt. vanilla ice cream, softened

Mix together pumpkin, brown sugar, cinnamon, ginger, cloves, and salt. Fold into softened ice cream. Pour mixture into chilled gingersnap crust. Cover and freeze.

CREAMY PUMPKIN PIE

- *A cool and creamy dessert.*

1 c. plain canned pumpkin
1/2 c. cold milk
1 large pkg. (5.1 oz.) vanilla instant
    pudding mix
1 tsp. pumpkin pie spice
1 container (8 oz.) whipped topping
9" graham cracker pie crust

Combine pumpkin, milk, pudding mix, and pie spice. Blend well. Fold in whipped topping. Spoon mixture into the graham cracker crust and chill. Garnish with dollops of whipped topping to serve.

PUMPKIN BREAD IN A JAR

- *A clever way to "package" a gift of bread.*

2/3 c. butter or margarine
2 3/4 c. granulated sugar
2 c. plain canned pumpkin
4 eggs
3/4 c. water
3 1/2 c. flour
1/2 tsp. baking powder
2 tsp. baking soda
1 1/4 tsp. salt
1 tsp. cloves
1 tsp. cinnamon
3/4 c. nuts (opt.)

Cream together margarine and sugar. Mix in eggs, water, and pumpkin. Add dry ingredients and mix well. Add nuts if desired. Fill greased, wide mouth pint jars 1/2 full with mixture. Clean top edge of jars well. Bake at 350 degrees for 35-45 minutes until inserted toothpick comes out clean. Remove from oven. Place scalded canning jar lids onto clean rims and apply bands while bread is still hot. As the bread cools the jars will seal. Keep in refrigerator and eat within a week. Makes 8-9 wide mouth pints. *Note: This is **not** for home storage. The sealed lid is a novelty and will not allow for extended storage.*

PUMPKIN PIE SPICE

- *A great combination of spices for holiday baking.*

4 tsp. ground cinnamon
2 tsp. ground ginger
1 tsp. ground cloves
1/4 tsp. ground allspice

Combine all ingredients and store in an airtight container. Use in any recipe that calls for pumpkin pie spice, such as the Creamy Pumpkin Pie above.

DOUBLE-DIPPED PEARS

- *A luscious taste-tempting treat.*

     6 large, ripe pears
     1 large bag of wrapped caramels
     8-oz. dipping chocolate
     1/2 c. desired toppings (candy sprinkles,
          chopped nuts, crushed candy bars, etc.)

Unwrap caramels and melt in a double boiler over low heat. Holding the small end of a pear, gently dip large end into caramel, leaving approximately 1 1/2" of the top exposed. Let cool on waxed paper. Melt chocolate in a double boiler over low heat. Next, dip pear into chocolate up to approximately 1" below where the caramel ended. (The pear should look layered from the top, with pear, caramel, and chocolate.) Immediately dip pear in chosen topping to coat 1/2 of the chocolate layer. Cool on waxed paper. Enjoy!

STUFFED PUMPKIN DINNER

- *Your family will love dinner served this way.*

Wash and dry a pumpkin. Cut a lid in the top of pumpkin and remove fibrous pulp and seeds. Prick the inside of the pumpkin with a fork. Place a hearty stew or a casserole in the pumpkin cavity and place on a cookie sheet. (Pre-cook any meat used.) Bake at 350 degrees until casserole is done and pumpkin is tender. To serve, scoop out the pumpkin along with the stew or casserole.

PEANUT BUTTER POPCORN

- *This is for peanut butter lovers!*

     10-12 c. popped popcorn
     1 c. granulated sugar
     1 c. light corn syrup
     1 c. peanut butter
     1 tsp. vanilla

In a saucepan combine sugar and corn syrup. Stirring constantly, bring to a boil over medium heat for 3-4 minutes. Remove from heat and stir in peanut butter and vanilla. Pour over popped popcorn and stir well.

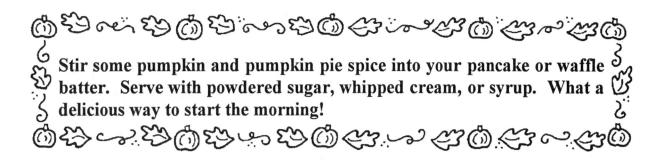

Stir some pumpkin and pumpkin pie spice into your pancake or waffle batter. Serve with powdered sugar, whipped cream, or syrup. What a delicious way to start the morning!

MOLDED BUTTER

- *Molded butter makes a wonderful gift when given with a basket of hot rolls.*

Butter or margarine can be molded into many holiday shapes. Plastic molds are sold at most craft and party stores for a minimal cost. Molds come in many shapes for every holiday. Butter shaped like a turkey is fun to serve for Thanksgiving dinner. You will receive many compliments from adults and children alike!

Soften margarine or butter at room temperature. Do not melt! Most molds take approximately 3/4 cup (1 1/2 cubes) margarine. Spoon margarine or butter into mold and press to fill all crevices. With a knife, level margarine across top of mold. Place in freezer until completely frozen. To remove from mold, gently pop out on a serving dish and you have a darling shaped butter.

FLAVORED BUTTERS

- *Use these butters as you would jam or jelly on your favorite bread.*

CRANBERRY BUTTER

1/2 c. fresh cranberries
1 3/4 c. powdered sugar
1/2 c. butter or margarine
1 Tbs. orange juice

Puree cranberries and sugar in blender. Add butter and orange juice and blend until smooth. Place in mold or serving dish and chill until firm.

CINNAMON BUTTER

1/2 c. butter or margarine
1 c. powdered sugar
1 1/2 tsp. cinnamon
2 tsp. milk

Cream butter and sugar. Add cinnamon and milk and mix well. Makes 1 cup.

FRUIT BUTTER

1 c. butter or margarine
2 Tbs. fruit flavored gelatin

Soften butter or margarine to room temperature. Add gelatin and blend well.

HONEY BUTTER

3/4 c. butter or margarine
1 1/2 c. honey
1 tsp. vanilla

Soften butter or margarine to room temperature. Place all ingredients in blender and whip until well blended. Serve with hot bread or rolls. (To make **honey-lemon butter**, substitute the vanilla a for 1 teaspoon grated lemon zest.)

HERB BUTTER

1/2 c. butter or margarine, softened
1 Tbs. dried or fresh minced herbs

Combine herbs and margarine and mix well. Shape if desired and chill. Serve with vegetables or hot bread.

HARVEST CHEESE

- *A block or wedge of cheese covered with fall leaves makes a perfect gift to take to the hostess of your Thanksgiving dinner.*

Gather attractive, non-toxic leaves (strawberry, maple, grape, raspberry, rose, aspen, etc.), wash, and pat dry. Place between pages of a large book and let dry for several days. Use a wedge or block of solid cheese such as cheddar. Cheese with holes does not work well. Chill cheese well. Melt some paraffin wax over low heat (2 lbs. will do several blocks of cheese). Dip the backside of a leaf in the wax and press onto the brick of cheese. Continue to add leaves to the cheese on all sides. After applying leaves, grasp the block of cheese at one end and quickly dip in pan of melted paraffin. Hold and let paraffin harden. Dip opposite end in the same manner. Make sure entire block of cheese is coated. Continue to dip cheese alternating ends until 3 coats have been added. Paraffin coated cheese will keep several months in the refrigerator. Gently break away the paraffin to serve.

DELICIOUS FALL LEAVES

- *Use leaf-shaped cookie cutters to create a touch of the season.*

Pie Dough Leaves
Purchase or prepare homemade pie crust pastry. Roll pastry to approximately 1/4" thickness. Using different leaf-shaped cookie cutters, cut out leaves and place on a cookie sheet. Sprinkle with cinnamon sugar and bake until golden brown for a delicious fall treat. Use pie dough leaves to cover the top of a pie instead of a plain crust, bake, and you will have a fancy dessert.

Tortilla Leaves
Using cookie cutters, cut leaves out of flour tortilla shells. Deep-fry leaves in oil until golden brown. Sprinkle with powdered or cinnamon sugar. If you do not wish to deep-fry, place tortilla leaves on a broiler pan, brush with oil, and sprinkle with cinnamon sugar. Broil until light brown and crisp.

Cookie Leaves
Children love to frost and decorate sugar cookies. Make Thanksgiving shapes such as leaves, turkeys, or pumpkins. Decorate cookies with colored icing, fall candies, colored sugar, or dried fruits and nuts. Try adding food coloring and flavoring to dough for extra variety. Our favorites are yellow with lemon flavoring and orange with orange flavoring. Cocoa may also be added for a chocolate flavor. Add almond extract for extra zip.

Cut cookie leaves from your favorite **shortbread** recipe. Bake and sprinkle with granulated sugar to make a melt-in-your-mouth cookie for fall. Fill a basket with these leaves and watch them disappear!

Chocolate Leaves
To make chocolate leaves for garnishing holiday desserts, melt dipping chocolate in a double boiler. Pour a layer of melted chocolate about 1/8" thick on waxed paper that has been spread on a cookie sheet. Freeze until set, about 5-10 minutes. Using cookie cutters, cut out leaves. Gently pull away waxed paper and remove leaves. Freeze until ready to serve.

GOBBLE SNACKS

• *Use one of these darling turkeys at each place setting.*

For **each** turkey you will need:

    1 chocolate candy kiss, unwrapped
    6 candy corns
    1 caramel
    1 red cinnamon candy (opt.)
    1 round cracker or cookie
    Royal Icing

Spread each cracker with Royal Icing (recipe page 102). Press an unwrapped chocolate kiss into the icing, placing it slightly below the center of the cracker. This will form the body of the turkey. Attach an unwrapped caramel to the back of the cracker with icing to help prop up the turkey. Press 5 candy corns into the icing above the kiss, large end up, to form the feathers. Attach a candy corn with icing, small end forward on top of the kiss to form the head. Place a red cinnamon candy to the side of the "head" to make the turkey wattle.

Make a fun fall wreath by cutting dried Indian corn into 2" - 3" pieces. Thread pieces on a piece of heavy duty wire and twist ends together to make a wreath. Add a raffia bow.

A BUNDLE OF BREADSTICKS

• *Take a bundle to your neighbor!*

Use frozen bread dough (thawed), or your own bread recipe. Roll bread dough into small ropes as long as a cookie sheet. Lay dough ropes on a greased cookie sheet approximately 1 1/2" apart. Spread with melted butter and sprinkle with poppy seeds, grated parmesan cheese, sesame seeds, garlic or onion salt, chives, etc. Let rise 30 minutes. Bake 10-15 minutes or until golden brown. Cool. If giving as a gift, tie a large bow around a bundle of breadsticks for an extra special touch.

GRAPEVINE WREATHS

• *Decorate your home with grapevines!*

Soak dry grapevines in water for about 45 minutes. (A great place to soak vines is in a bathtub.) To make a wreath, firmly wrap the soaked vines around a bucket or a large can. Continue to wrap vines until desired thickness is reached. Secure vines in place with wire or jute. Remove wreath from the bucket or can and let dry for several days. Other grapevine shapes can also be made by wrapping the vines around various shaped objects. Decorate dry grapevine wreaths as desired.

TURKEY HANDS

- *Children have a great time making these hand-shaped cookies.*

Roll out sugar cookie or gingerbread dough to approximately 1/4" thickness. Have a child place a hand on the dough. Cut around the child's hand making a "handprint" shape from dough. Place on a greased cookie sheet and bake according to recipe. The hand shape resembles a turkey with the "thumb" being the head and the "fingers" being four feathers. Have icing and a variety of candies available for each child to decorate their turkeys. This will bring a lot of smiles and creativity!

CRANBERRY SPICE PUNCH

- *A wonderful drink to warm you on those cool fall nights!*

> 1 gallon cran-raspberry or cran-apple
> drink
> 5 whole cloves
> 3 cinnamon sticks

Heat drink with cloves and cinnamon sticks. Simmer for 10-15 minutes on low. Remove cloves and cinnamon sticks and serve hot. This is also delicious chilled and served cold.

SOFT CARAMEL DIP

- *A melt-in-your-mouth dip for fruit.*

> 50 wrapped caramels (approximately)
> 1 pkg. (8 oz.) cream cheese
> 1 c. sour cream

Unwrap and melt caramels over low heat in a double boiler. Combine cream cheese and sour cream and mix well. Stir into caramel. Serve as a dip for apples, oranges, strawberries, or any other fruit chunks desired.

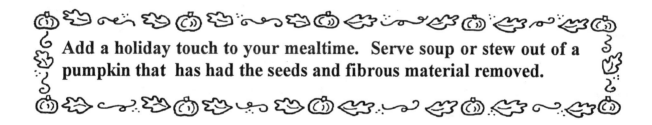

Add a holiday touch to your mealtime. Serve soup or stew out of a pumpkin that has had the seeds and fibrous material removed.

PAINTED PINECONES

- *Fill a basket with an array of fall colors.*

Spray paint pinecones of various sizes with vibrant fall colors. Arrange the pinecones in a large wicker basket. Tie a raffia bow onto the handle of the basket. Set the basket on a hearth or use for a centerpiece.

HARVEST CENTERPIECES

- *Ideas to create a beautiful Thanksgiving table.*

Harvest Candle Holders
To make harvest candle holders, bore a candle-sized hole in small pumpkins or gourds. Gourds come in many interesting shapes and colors. Insert a candle so it fits snugly. (Use a small piece of PVC pipe to firmly hold candle in the gourd if necessary.) If needed, slice a small area off the bottom of the gourds to allow stability.

Blooming Apples
Make a small hole in the top of several red apples. Insert a marigold blossom into each hole. Cut marigold stems short so the blossom is flush against the apple. Pile the apples in a basket for a colorful display.

Plaid Tied Apples
Fill a basket with large apples that have stems. On each stem, tie a plaid ribbon bow. This is a fun gift to give a teacher with a note of thanks.

Potato Base for Foliage
You may be surprised at the amount of greenery you can collect from your yard to create a centerpiece. Cut stems of evergreen bushes and trees, holly, colorful leaves, marigolds, mums, and twigs. Insert stems into a potato to use as a solid base. Be sure to add enough foliage to hide potato. Add a bow and you will have a dazzling arrangement!

Pumpkin Arrangement
Hollow out a medium-sized pumpkin and insert a piece of floral foam in the base. Arrange fresh or dried greenery, flowers, and leaves in the pumpkin shell. A large bundle of wheat tied with a raffia bow also looks nice.

Gold Elegance
A can of gold spray paint can be a great decorating tool! Spray dry leaves of various shapes and sizes, then sprinkle them down the center of a table or put them under a centerpiece. Pumpkins and gourds look beautiful sprayed gold. Spray nuts in the shell, dried pomegranates, twigs, and silk or plastic flowers. It is amazing what beauty and elegance this will create.

To add some gold sparkle to your fall arrangement, try this unique idea. Gently pry apart 5 walnuts. Glue a floral wire of desired length to the 1/2 inside shell and glue the second half of the shell to the first. Wrap wire with floral tape. Spray the walnuts with gold spray paint. Assemble a spray of 5 walnuts together. Make as many of these sprays as needed.

Sprinkle acorns and colorful fall leaves down the center of the table. Add mini pumpkins and gourds among the leaves.

HARVEST SNOWMAN

- *A fun way to decorate a snowman and a way to provide a treat for the birds.*

Make a snowman using three large snowballs. Use branches or twigs to make arms. For buttons, use pinecones dipped in peanut butter and birdseed. Use a carrot for a nose, dried prunes for the eyes, and raisins for the mouth. String popcorn, raisins, and cranberries on a strong thread using a needle to push through each item. Wrap around the snowman several times to make a belt or a sash. To add the finishing touch, place an old hat on the snowman's head. Fill the hat brim with sunflower seeds, birdseed, and popcorn. Enjoy watching the birds feast!

BIRDSEED WREATH

- *Present a harvest feast for the birds.*

Using frozen (thawed) or homemade bread dough, make a wreath by forming two ropes of dough of equal length (approximately 2 1/2 feet each). Twist the two ropes together and form into a circle. Pinch ends together and place on a greased cookie sheet. Let rise till double. Bake until golden brown. Remove from oven and brush liberally with beaten egg white. Sprinkle birdseed on wreath immediately after egg white is applied so it will stick. Bake for 2 more minutes and remove from oven. Let dry for 2-3 days until hard. Add a bow if desired. Hang with wire on a door or fence so the birds can enjoy.

PAPER BAG CORNUCOPIA

- *A great way to display fresh fruit.*

Take a brown paper bag (large or small depending on size needed) and fold top down about 2". Fold down once more to create a rim. Gradually gather bag between both hands and twist bottom end of the bag into a tight twist resembling the tip of a cornucopia (horn of plenty). You may need to tack areas of the bag with a hot glue to help hold the twist in place. Spray with brown or gold spray paint. Allow to dry and display an array of fresh fruit from the opening. *Note:* Flat lightweight paper sacks work best. You may also use newspaper, kraft, or butcher paper by making a large cone and twisting it in the same manner as a paper bag.

PICTURE PLACE CARDS

- *A picture can say a thousand words.*

Instead of the usual place cards used at Thanksgiving dinner to indicate where family members and guests are to be seated, try this fun idea! Either take or obtain a snapshot of each guest or family member coming to dinner. (You may need to gradually take pictures several months ahead of time so as to have a picture of everyone.) Cut around the photo and glue to a place card without writing a name on it. When it is time for guests to be seated, they must look for their photo to find a place. This can be a lot of fun and a great conversation piece. Photos that are creative (such as Uncle Tom laying out at the beach, or Grandma skiing) tend to be the most fun!

TREASURED TABLECLOTHS

- *Create a one-of-a-kind tablecloth to use each year.*

Try one of the following ideas for creating a special holiday tablecloth. Purchase or make a plain colored cotton or muslin tablecloth (white or cream colored works best). A flat sheet can also be used.

Inner Tube Stamp
Cut various leaf shapes from an old piece of rubber inner tube. Mount each shape onto a small wooden block with glue that will adhere to rubber. Place several fall colors of fabric paint onto different paper plates. Dip each "stamp" into the paint and press onto tablecloth. Alternate colors and continue to stamp entire cloth. Let dry well. You will have a festive harvest tablecloth to use.

Signature Tablecloth
Have each guest or family member sign a tablecloth with a permanent marker or fabric pen. Make sure to date each name. Continue this tradition and you will enjoy remembering who was at Thanksgiving dinner each year! Another fun idea is to have guests apply their handprint above their name with fabric paint or fabric crayons.

Apple Printing
Cut an apple horizontally so a "star" shape is created. Dip cut side of apple in red fabric paint and gently blot on a paper plate to remove excess paint. Press onto cloth to print an apple shape. Cover entire cloth.

Stencilled Shapes
Use butcher paper for this. Make sure paper is long enough to cover your table with a little extra so ends can be taped under. Lay paper on a hard surface such as a floor. Take a purchased plastic stencil with a simple large fall shape such as a pumpkin or a leaf. (Homemade stencils can be made by cutting a simple shape out of thin cardstock.) Dip a sponge into fabric paint and sponge over stencil. Remove stencil to reveal shape. Continue to cover paper being creative with colors and shapes. This is a fun idea for any holiday or party and is disposable for easy clean up.

CANDY CORN FAVORS

- *A "sweet" place card.*

Purchase small 3" - 4" clay flower pots. Using acrylic paint, paint the rims a golden yellow, the middle sections orange and the lower 1/4 of the pots white. The pots should look like candy corn. Line pots with plastic wrap or foil. Fill with candy corn and paste a place card on a pipe cleaner and insert in the candy. Set one at each place setting.

THANKSGIVING THANKS

- *Clapping game of thanks.*

Have guests sit in a circle. Begin the game by instructing everyone to create a rhythm by first slapping knees, then clapping hands, then snapping fingers. Appoint someone to be first to say what they are thankful for as the fingers are snapped. Continue doing this rhythm and each time the fingers are snapped, the next person in the circle will say what they are thankful for. If a player misses a beat by not saying what they are thankful for they are out of the game. Continue playing in this manner.

ABC THANKS

- *A game for children to play when they are waiting for the turkey to cook.*

Have everyone sit in a circle. Start with the first person who begins, "I am thankful for...," and then must state something he is thankful for that begins with the letter "A." The next person begins the same, then states what the first person said and adds something he/she is thankful for that starts with the letter "B." This continues around the circle until the letter "Z" is reached. Hopefully the last person is someone with a good memory!

LENGTHS OF THANKS

- *A fun way to let everyone express thankfulness.*

Wind a skein of yarn into a ball. As you wind, cut various lengths of the yarn making some long and some short. Keep winding until yarn skein is gone and you have a ball with at least as many lengths as you have guests. When ready to begin, have the first person begin to unwind the yarn. The person must tell what he/she is thankful for and must keep talking until the piece of yarn ends. The ball of yarn is then passed to the next person and this continues until everyone has a chance to express thanks.

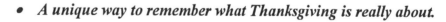

THANKFUL CAKE

- *A unique way to remember what Thanksgiving is really about.*

As guests arrive for Thanksgiving dinner, have them write on a slip of paper something they are grateful for and sign their name. Fold each paper small and wrap in foil. Have a previously baked cake ready to frost. Make small slits throughout the cake and insert a foil-wrapped note into each slit. Try to distribute evenly. Frost cake. When dessert is served, have each person read aloud the gratitude note found in his/her piece of cake. Make sure all notes are read.

MR. TURKEY PUMPKIN PICKS

- *Want the cutest pumpkin on the block? Try this!*

> 1/2" thick pine board (cut body, feathers, and beak)
> 1/4" thick pine board (cut wattle)
> 1/4" dowel sticks (3 feet total)
> Acrylic paint (light brown, yellow, red, black,
>   white, green, burgundy, blue)
> 1 bandana
> Wood glue
> 1 medium-sized pumpkin

1. Enlarge pattern as needed according to your pumpkin size. Trace pattern (or freehand) onto wood. With a band or scroll saw, cut body, feathers, and beak from the 1/2" pine board and the wattle from the 1/4" pine board. Sand all cut pieces until smooth.
2. With acrylic paint, paint the body piece light brown, the wattle and one feather red, the beak and one feather yellow, and the remaining feathers green, blue, and burgundy respectively (or whatever color combination you desire).
3. Trace the eyes on the head and paint white and black according to pattern. Add black accents on beak. Lightly stipple cheeks red.
4. Using an old toothbrush, lightly fleck black paint over all pieces. Lightly sand around the edges of the painted pieces letting some of the natural wood show through.
5. Cut dowels in approximately 6" lengths. Sand one end of each dowel piece (or place in pencil sharpener) to a point. Drill a 1/4" wide hole (approximately 1" deep) in the center bottom of the body and each feather piece. Glue the blunt end of each dowel piece into a drilled hole. Glue the beak and wattle onto the head (body piece). Let dry well.

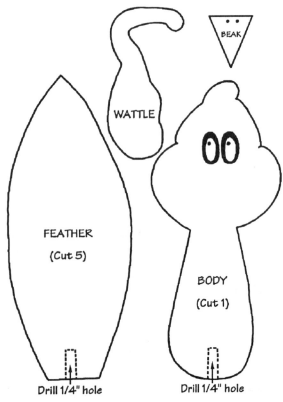

To assemble:
Assemble turkey as shown in illustration (above). Remember to place the wood pieces in the uncarved pumpkin where you want them the first time so they will hold up well and not wobble from too many holes being poked. Tie the bandana around the base of the body piece where it meets the pumpkin. Use pumpkin picks year after year.

Note: If pumpkin will be used outside, you may wish to paint the wood pieces with weather proof paint and sealer. If pattern is enlarged for an extra large pumpkin, use 1" thick pine board instead of the 1/2".

CHRISTMAS

RIBBON BREAD

- *An elegant gift of bread.*

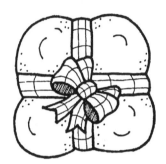

    1 loaf frozen bread dough (or homemade)
    Melted butter or margarine
    20" x 1 1/2" brown paper strip
    15" x 1 1/2" brown paper strip
    4 paper clips
    Christmas ribbon, 1 1/2" wide

Let frozen bread dough thaw. Allow to rise once and then punch down. (Optional, knead spices, raisins, nuts, dried fruits, etc. into dough.) Shape dough into an 8" x 5" rectangle. Generously grease a cookie sheet and place the paper strips perpendicular to each other on the sheet. Brush the strips with melted butter. Center the shaped dough over the strips. Wrap the strips loosely around the dough so you can place two fingers underneath them. Secure together with paper clips. Let the dough rise in a warm place until doubled (do not let dough rise too much). Bake at 350 degrees for 40 minutes or until golden brown. Let bread cool on a wire rack. Remove paper strips and wrap with ribbon in the indentions where the paper strips were. Tie a bow on top and you have a beautiful "gift" of bread.

ROYAL ROCKY ROAD FUDGE

- *Fudge fit for a king!*

    1 pkg. (12 oz.) semi-sweet chocolate
        chips
    1 c. butter
    4 c. granulated sugar
    1 1/2 c. evaporated milk
    20 large marshmallows
    1 1/2 c. walnut pieces
    2 c. miniature marshmallows
    20 maraschino cherries, halved

Place miniature marshmallows in freezer. In a large bowl, cut butter into chocolate chips. Set aside. In a saucepan add evaporated milk, sugar, and the 20 large marshmallows. Stirring constantly, boil over medium heat for five minutes. Pour over butter and chocolate chip mixture. Stir until mixture melts and starts to thicken. Add frozen miniature marshmallows, nuts, and cherries. Pour into a buttered 9" x 13" pan. Refrigerate until set. Cut and serve.

HOLIDAY WASSAIL

- *A warm, comforting drink.*

3 qts. apple cider
3 c. orange juice
3 c. pineapple juice
3/4 c. lemon juice
3/4 c. granulated sugar
16 whole cloves
4-6 cinnamon sticks

In a large pan mix ingredients together and bring to a boil. Reduce heat and simmer for 15 minutes. Remove cloves and cinnamon sticks. Serve warm. If desired, float orange slices studded with cloves or place dollops of whipped topping in the wassail. Makes about 5 quarts.

PERFECT PEPPERMINT EGGNOG

- *Serve this creamy eggnog at your holiday party.*

1/2 gallon pink peppermint ice cream
2 qts. eggnog
2-3 qts. lemon-lime soda
Whipping cream, whipped
Peppermint candies, crushed

Add ice cream to punch bowl. Add eggnog and mix well. Add the lemon-lime soda. (A few drops of red food coloring may be added to make a nice pink color.) Garnish with dollops of whipped cream and crushed peppermint candies. Yum!

CANDY APPLE CIDER

- *A punch to warm the soul.*

3/4 c. red cinnamon candies
1 c. lemon juice
2 qts. apple cider or apple juice
1/3 c. brown sugar
20 whole cloves
5 red apples, cored and sliced into rings (opt.)

Melt cinnamon candies with lemon juice over low heat. Add apple cider, sugar, and cloves. Simmer for 20 minutes. Remove the cloves and serve. Use apple rings as garnish (see tip box below).

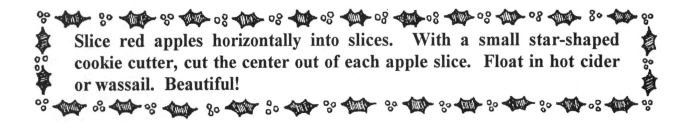

Slice red apples horizontally into slices. With a small star-shaped cookie cutter, cut the center out of each apple slice. Float in hot cider or wassail. Beautiful!

GOURMET CANDY APPLES

- *A beautiful gift! Decorate for any holiday throughout the year.*

   Large red apples
   Wrapped caramels or homemade caramel
   Dipping chocolate or semi-sweet summer coating
   Vanilla flavored almond bark or vanilla flavored summer coating
   Assorted toppings: chopped nuts (any and all kinds),
         granola, raisins, dried fruits, coconut, crushed
         graham crackers, toffee, M&M brand candies (seasonal
   colors), crushed candy bars of any kind, marshmallows, small candies, etc.

Unwrap and melt caramels over low heat in a double boiler. Homemade caramel may also be used (see recipe below). Melt dipping chocolate and vanilla flavored almond bark in separate containers in the microwave on medium heat stirring every 30 seconds.

Insert a fork into the top of an apple (at room temperature) to use as a handle while preparing. Spread melted caramel over 1/2 of the apple and immediately roll in nuts or topping of your choice. Do the same on the other side of the apple. (You will need to place apple in the freezer on a small plate for a few minutes between each layer to help set the caramel and the chocolate.) Next drizzle or spread more caramel over the entire apple and roll in a different topping. Drizzle chocolate over apple and add more toppings. Next, drizzle vanilla flavored almond bark over apple and add more toppings. Continue layers until apple has approximately 1" of toppings.   Apple will keep up to two weeks in the refrigerator.

This gourmet apple makes a wonderful gift! It can be made for any holiday or special occasion. Pick candies and toppings to coordinate with the holiday. Wrap the finished apples in cellophane and tie with ribbons, raffia, holiday picks, etc.   Neighbors will give you rave reviews for this unique gift! Give one to your child's teacher with a tag that states, "A gourmet apple for a gourmet teacher!" Don't forget to add the cutting directions for serving (below). Use your imagination and have fun.

To cut and serve apple: Cut apple into quarters and remove the seeds and core. Next cut each quarter crosswise into wedge-shaped pieces.   The gourmet apple is a rich dessert and will serve approximately 6 people.

HOMEMADE CARAMEL

   1 1/2 c. granulated sugar
   1 1/2 c. brown sugar
   1 1/2 c. butter
   1 1/2 c. light corn syrup
   1 can (14 oz.) sweetened condensed milk

Combine ingredients in a heavy sauce pan. Stirring constantly, bring to a boil. Cook until mixture reaches 238 degrees or forms a firm ball when added to cold water. Use as a caramel coating for candy apples or use to make wrapped caramels by pouring into a greased 9" x 13" pan and cooling overnight. Cut and wrap in waxed paper if desired.

FLAMING CARROT PUDDING

- *Light up your holidays and impress your friends!*

Batter

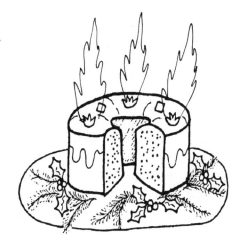

1 c. grated carrots	1 3/4 c. flour
1/2 c. brown sugar, firmly packed	1 tsp. baking powder
1 egg	1 tsp. soda
1 tsp. grated orange zest	1/2 tsp. salt
1 tsp. grated lemon zest	1/2 tsp. cloves
1 Tbs. lemon juice	1 tsp. cinnamon
4 Tbs. margarine, softened	1/2 c. chopped nuts

Syrup

1 c. granulated sugar
1 1/2 c. water
1 1/2 c. golden raisins

Mix batter ingredients in order given. Place syrup ingredients together in a saucepan and bring to a boil. Grease well a large bundt pan. Pour hot syrup mixture into the bottom of the bundt pan. Carefully spoon batter evenly over top of syrup. Do not stir. Bake at 400 degrees for 45 minutes or until a toothpick inserted comes out clean. Remove from oven and turn out on serving plate. Sauce with raisins will be on top of pudding. Garnish with maraschino cherries. Serve hot. Serves 8-10.

To flame pudding:
Soak sugar cubes in lemon extract until saturated. Place several cubes around the top of the pudding. When ready to serve, light the sugar cubes with a match and cubes will flame.

PIÑA COLADA BREAD

- *A taste of the tropics.*

4 eggs	3 c. flour
1 1/4 c. oil	1 tsp. salt
2 c. granulated sugar	1 tsp. soda
1 tsp. coconut extract	1 tsp. cinnamon
1 tsp. orange extract	1 can (20 oz.) crushed pineapple, drained
1 tsp. vanilla	1/2 c. flaked coconut
1/4 c. pineapple juice	1/2 c. maraschino cherries, chopped
1/2 tsp. grated orange zest	1/2 c. macadamia nuts, chopped

Beat eggs and stir in oil and sugar. Add vanilla, extracts, pineapple juice, and orange zest. In a separate bowl, sift together dry ingredients. Add to egg mixture and stir just until ingredients are moistened. Gently stir in crushed pineapple, coconut, maraschino cherries, and nuts. Pour into loaf pans that have been greased and floured well. Bake at 350 degrees for 45-50 minutes or until a toothpick inserted comes out clean. Let cool in pan for 10 minutes then remove.

REINDEER MUNCHIES

- *A yummy snack for all your little "deers."*

        3 c. Bugles brand nacho cheese snacks
        1 1/4 c. toasted oat cereal
        2 c. pretzels
        3 c. popped popcorn
        1/2 c. chow mein noodles
        1/2 c. melted margarine
        1/2 tsp. chili powder
        1/4 tsp. garlic powder

Combine first 5 ingredients in a large bowl. Mix together margarine and spices. Pour over popcorn mixture and toss to coat well. Spread mixture onto an ungreased cookie sheet and bake uncovered for 15 minutes at 300 degrees. Stir several times during baking. Cool. Store covered at room temperature.

SNOW ICE CREAM

- *A treat from the great outdoors.*

        8 c. loose clean snow
        5 Tbs. milk
        3/4 c. granulated sugar
        2 1/4 tsp. vanilla

Mix ingredients together well. Add more sugar if needed for taste. Serve.

PEPPERMINT MERINGUES

- *A delicious no fat treat.*

        2 large egg whites (room temperature)
        1/8 tsp. cream of tartar
        1/8 tsp. salt
        1/2 c. granulated sugar
        3 large peppermint candy canes, crushed

Beat egg whites, cream of tartar, and salt with an electric mixer until soft peaks form. Gradually add sugar and beat mixture for approximately 5 minutes or until mixture is glossy and smooth in texture. Drop by teaspoonfuls onto foil covered cookie sheets, approximately 1" apart. Sprinkle the crushed candy canes over the tops of the meringues. Bake at 225 degrees for 1 1/2 hours. The meringues will look white and dry when done. Turn off the oven and let the meringues cool with oven door ajar. Store in a cool dry place. Yield approximately 50 meringues.

To make **wreath meringues**, omit the candy canes and add 1/4 tsp. mint extract and a few drops of green food color. Spoon meringue into a pastry bag with a star or round decorating tip. Pipe two 1 1/2" circles of the meringue, one on top of each other. Decorate wreaths with tiny bits of red and green candied cherries. Bake wreaths as for peppermint meringues.

HOT CHOCOLATE SPOONS

- *Stir rich flavor into hot chocolate.*

Melt a small amount of semi-sweet dipping chocolate and white chocolate over low heat in separate double boilers. Dip the round end of a spoon (heavy duty plastic spoons can be used) in either the semi-sweet or white chocolate several times. Place on waxed paper between coats. Drizzle with the opposite color of chocolate that spoons were originally dipped in. Sprinkle with a tiny amount of crushed peppermint or dip in colored sugars if desired. Let set until firm. Use to stir hot chocolate.

CINNAMON MILK MIX

- *Perfect for a cold snowy day.*

  2 c. powdered milk
  1 Tbs. cinnamon
  1 c. powdered non-dairy creamer
  1 1/4 c. granulated sugar

Mix ingredients together well. Store in a covered container. To use, add 1/3 cup of mix and 1 cup hot water in a mug. Stir well. A few drops of vanilla can be added for extra flavor.

This mix makes a great gift for a neighbor or co-worker. Put mix in a plastic bag and tie top with a ribbon. Make a simple fabric bag, put in mix and tie top with jute. Add directions on how to use the mix. Tie some cinnamon sticks with the jute for an extra holiday touch.

CHRISTMAS MOUSSE

- *"Merry Chrismoose."*

  1 large pkg. (5.9 oz.) chocolate fudge
        instant pudding mix
  1 pkg. Dream Whip brand topping mix
  2 c. milk

Mix the pudding mix and Dream Whip with the 2 cups of milk and beat until thick. Refrigerate until set. Before serving, remove mixture from refrigerator and beat until fluffy. Serves 6-8.

CANDY CANE CRUNCH

- *A melt-in-your-mouth treat.*

  2 lbs. vanilla flavored almond bark
  1/2 lb. crushed peppermint candy canes

Melt almond bark in a double boiler over low heat, stirring constantly. Remove from heat and add the crushed peppermint candy canes. Line a cookie sheet with waxed paper and pour the candy over the paper and spread out over the sheet. Place in refrigerator to chill. Break into pieces and store in an air tight container.

SPUN CINNAMON POPCORN

- *If you like cinnamon, you will love this!*

  1 c. butter or margarine
  1/2 c. light corn syrup
  1 pkg. (9 oz.) red cinnamon candies
  8 qts. popped popcorn

Combine butter, corn syrup, and cinnamon candies in a heavy saucepan. Bring to a boil over medium heat, stirring constantly. Boil for 5 minutes. Pour over popcorn and mix well. Pour onto a greased cookie sheet and spread out. Bake at 275 degrees for 1 hour. Stir several times while baking. Remove from oven and allow to cool. Break apart. Store in an airtight container.

LAYERED COOKIE MIX

- *A perfect gift to give during the holidays.*

Choose your favorite cookie recipe (any recipe will work but those that have nuts, raisins, candies, and/or chocolate chips look best). Layer the **dry** ingredients in a clear jar. Add a bow or decorate the lid as desired. Copy the cookie recipe onto a card and include with the mix. Add instructions as to what wet ingredients must be added and the cooking time to complete the cookies.

DIPPED PRETZEL RODS

- *A chocolate and caramel treat.*

    1 pkg. (10 oz.) large pretzel rods
    1 lb. dipping chocolate or semi-sweet summer coating
    1 lb. wrapped caramels
    Vanilla flavored almond bark or vanilla flavored summer
        coating
    Small candy sprinkles or chopped nuts (opt.)

Melt dipping chocolate and unwrapped caramels in separate double boilers. Dip each pretzel rod 3/4 of the way into the caramel and let set on waxed paper until caramel is firm. Next dip the rod in the melted chocolate half-way up the rod and let set on waxed paper. After the chocolate is firm, melt the vanilla flavored almond bark in the microwave on medium heat or in a double boiler. Drizzle with a spoon over the semi-sweet chocolate. (If desired roll the rods in candy sprinkles or chopped nuts immediately after dipping it into the chocolate omitting the drizzle.)

CHOCOLATE CANES

- *Make a gourmet candy cane.*

Melt vanilla flavored almond bark over low heat in a double boiler. With tongs, dip a candy cane partially in the melted almond bark. Let set on waxed paper. When almond bark is set, dip other end of the candy cane so entire cane is coated. Let set on waxed paper. Melt a small amount of semi-sweet chocolate chips. (Add shortening to thin if necessary.) With a spoon, drizzle the melted chocolate chips over the dipped canes to decorate. Canes can also be dipped in semi-sweet chocolate and drizzled with the vanilla flavored almond bark. For a gift, fill a Christmas tin full!

GUMDROP FUDGE

- *This holiday fudge is great for a last minute gift.*

    3 c. granulated sugar
    3/4 c. margarine
    2/3 c. evaporated milk
    1 jar (7 oz.) marshmallow creme
    1 pkg. (12 oz.) semi-sweet chocolate chips
    1 tsp. vanilla
    1 c. small red and green gumdrops
    1 c. nuts, chopped (opt.)

Combine sugar, margarine, and milk in a heavy saucepan. Over medium heat, bring to a boil. Stirring constantly, boil for 5 minutes or until mixture reaches 234 degrees. Remove from heat and stir in chocolate chips. When chocolate is melted, add the marshmallow creme, vanilla, nuts, and gumdrops. Stir well. Pour mixture into a greased 8" x 12" pan. Cool and cut into small squares.

CANDY WREATHS

- *An edible wreath to be gradually eaten throughout the holidays.*

Using heavy wire or a clothes hanger, form a circle 10" - 12" in diameter. Cover the entire wire ring with wrapped holiday candies. To attach candies, use a long piece of thin craft wire. Wrap wire around the end of each candy and then wrap on wire ring to secure. Continue to attach candies close together until entire ring is covered. Add a bow and a pair of scissors so pieces of candy can be cut off and eaten.

ROYAL ICING

- *An icing that hardens as it dries. Perfect for decorating holiday creations throughout the year.*

3 egg whites
1 1b. powdered sugar
1/2 tsp. cream of tartar
food coloring (opt.)

To make icing, mix ingredients and beat with an electric mixer on high speed for 7-10 minutes. Keep covered to prevent drying. Does not re-whip.

GRAHAM CRACKER HOUSE

- *A great family tradition.*

7 graham cracker squares
Assorted small holiday candies
Colored sugar and candy sprinkles (opt.)
Royal Icing (above)

To make a graham cracker "gingerbread house," use 4 graham crackers for the walls and one for the base. Attach the edges of the crackers together using the icing as you would glue. Spread icing with a knife or use a pastry bag. Attach two crackers on top of the walls to form the roof. (Triangular pieces can be cut from a graham cracker and attached to end walls to hold roof if desired.) Set the house on a plate or a piece of cardboard covered with foil and secure with icing. Allow the house to dry before decorating. Decorate the graham cracker house by attaching small candies with icing. Use candy sprinkles or colored sugar if desired. When finished, sprinkle a fine dust of powdered sugar over your house to make it look like snow. Kids love this project! *Note:* "Gingerbread houses" can be made using store bought cookies. Look in the cookie isle for fun varieties and shapes of cookies. Be creative!

Make small cookie wreaths by overlapping cut-out sugar cookies on a cookie sheet to form a circle. Bake and cookies will adhere together.

102

SANTA HAT JAR TOPPER

- *Ho Ho Ho - What a nice gift!*

Take a women's red sock (crew style) and place a small piece of polyester stuffing in the toe. Tie a bow around the end of the sock just above the stuffing. Tie on a jingle bell and a piece of holly. Roll cuff of sock down twice and place over the lid of the jar. The jar looks like it is wearing a stocking cap! Fill the jar with some fun items such as holiday candies, thoughts, small toys, coins, or candy canes. A stocking hat jar topper adds a special holiday touch to a gift of home canned fruits, vegetables, jams, jellies, or other gifts from your kitchen.

REINDEER ROOT BEER

- *A perfect gift for a child to make and give.*

To make these reindeer, purchase brown, glass bottles of root beer such as IBC brand. This brand comes in large or small bottles that have skinny necks.

To decorate, twist a large fuzzy brown pipe cleaner around the top of the bottle just under the cap, so an equal amount of pipe cleaner sticks out on either side. Cut another brown pipe cleaner in half. Twist one of the pieces of cut pipe cleaner around the pipe cleaner on the bottle, about 2" down from top (see illustration). You should now have three "prongs" forming one of the antlers. Repeat on other side. Glue two wiggly craft eyes below the antlers. Glue on a red pom-pom nose and tie a ribbon around the "neck" or below the antlers of the reindeer. Attach a gift tag for gift giving.

FRAGRANT CINNAMON ORNAMENTS

- *Fill your home with the scents of Christmas.*

    6 Tbs. applesauce
    10 Tbs. ground cinnamon
    1 tsp. ground cloves

Mix together all ingredients to form a dough. If dough is dry, add more applesauce. Roll out dough to approximately 1/8" thick on a cinnamon sprinkled surface. Cut dough into desired holiday shapes using cookie cutters. Cut a hole in the top of each shape with a drinking straw large enough to thread a ribbon through for hanging. To make details on shapes, use a toothpick to make indentions and designs. Place cinnamon shapes on a cookie sheet or cake rack. Place in a 150 degree oven or the lowest setting for 2 hours. Turn oven off and leave shapes in oven 5-6 hours or overnight. Tie ribbons through holes and use as ornaments or tie on packages. Store in airtight containers.

CANDY FILLED REINDEER

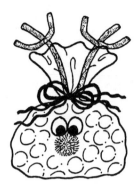

- *Change the look of the reindeer by filling with different types of candies.*

Cut a square piece of cellophane approximately 24" x 24". Place holiday candies (wrapped peppermints, malt balls, gumdrops, etc.) in the center of the cellophane. Add enough candies to make a large popcorn ball size. Gather up the cellophane around candy and tie with a bow. Tie on a jingle bell. Glue on wiggly craft eyes (3/4") and a red pom-pom nose (1/2"). Use 2 brown pipe cleaners to make antlers (wrap smaller pieces on the ends to form 3 points). Poke antlers down between gathers of cellophane and tack with hot glue. Use scissors and trim cellophane if needed. Add a tag for gift giving.

"SOUPER" HOLIDAY GIFT

- *A delicious gift idea.*

You will need 6 cans of soup to make this "souper" gift. Place a 1" wide ribbon several feet long on a table. Place three cans, lying on their sides in the center of the ribbon, side by side. Place two more cans on top of the first and one more on top. You should have a small pyramid. Wrap the ribbon tightly around the pyramid of cans so it forms a Christmas tree shape from the side. If desired, decorate the ends of the cans with holiday stickers. Attach a tag that states, "Have a *souper* Christmas!" For an extra creative touch, cover the soup labels with green holiday wrapping paper before stacking.

ICE CREAM CONE TREES

- *Decorate your table with an edible forest.*

Cover a cookie sheet with waxed paper. Invert sugar cones (pointed ice cream cones) onto the cookie sheet with the pointed ends up. Frost each cone entirely with green-tinted icing, flavored with mint extract. Decorate "trees" with gumdrops, popped corn, or small candies. Make sure to add a piece of candy to the top of the cone. Allow to dry. Place one cone at each place setting for a Christmas favor.

SANTA HATS

- *Leave a plateful for the jolly old elf himself!*

Coat Bugles brand corn snacks with melted, vanilla flavored almond bark. Sprinkle with red colored granulated sugar and let set on waxed paper. Attach a miniature marshmallow on the tip of each corn snack with the melted almond bark. These treats look like Santa hats.

CHOCOLATE PEPPERMINT CREAM PUFF RING

• *A beautiful and elegant dessert. A great choice when entertaining.*

Pastry	Filling
1/2 c. butter or margarine	1 qt. whipping cream
1 c. water	1/3 c. granulated sugar
1/4 tsp. salt	1/2 c. peppermint candies, finely crushed
1 c. flour	3 c. miniature marshmallows
4 eggs	4 drops red food coloring

Melt butter in a heavy saucepan. Add water and salt and bring to a boil. Remove from heat and add flour. Stir until mixture forms a ball and leaves the sides of the pan. Add eggs to the mixture one at a time, beating well after each. Mix until pastry is a soft and sticky batter.

Grease and flour a cookie sheet. Using a salad plate as a guide, trace a circle in the flour with a knife. Drop mounds of batter, touching each other, along circle to form a ring. Bake at 400 degrees for 45 minutes. Turn oven off and leave in oven for 15 more minutes. Remove and cool. Carefully cut pastry ring in half horizontally and scoop out and discard soft interior. This will create a hollow shell ready to add filling.

To prepare filling, whip the cream until soft peaks form. Add sugar to taste. Fold in crushed peppermint and marshmallows. Add red food coloring to create a nice pink color. Spoon into pastry ring and replace top. Fill immediately before serving. Drizzle top of ring with melted semi-sweet chocolate chips or frost with chocolate icing.

CHRISTMAS MICE

• *Unique chocolate maraschino cherry mouse.*

For **each** mouse you will need:

    1 maraschino cherry with stem
    1 chocolate candy kiss, unwrapped
    Semi-sweet dipping chocolate
    2 peanut halves
    3 silver dragées (candy decorating balls)

Melt a small amount of chocolate in a double boiler over low heat. Dip cherry into melted chocolate by holding stem. Place on a waxed paper covered tray. Immediately stick unwrapped flat end of the chocolate kiss onto end of chocolate covered cherry. Place the silver dragées (or other tiny round candies) into a tiny dot of chocolate then adhere them to the chocolate kiss for eyes and nose. Use a small amount of chocolate to adhere peanut halves between cherry and chocolate kiss to make the ears. Cool in refrigerator.

EGGNOG FRENCH TOAST

- *A great Christmas morning brunch with a flavor of eggnog.*

Cut bread into thick slices. Use any type of bread desired. Raisin bread, French bread, or white bread work well. Dip each side of the bread in a bowl of eggnog and allow to soak for several seconds. Place on griddle and cook each side until golden brown. Serve hot with butter and syrup. Yum!

BREAKFAST BOXES

- *A meal your family won't forget.*

Fill shoe boxes with simple breakfast foods such as fruit, bagels, muffins, small cans of juice, etc. Place lids on boxes and carefully wrap in gift wrap. Spread a tablecloth by the Christmas tree and place the "breakfast boxes" under the tree. What a fun surprise your family will have when breakfast is served.

CHRISTMAS MORNING CASSEROLE

- *Make this casserole the night before and bake the next morning.*

10 slices bread, cubed
2 1/4 c. grated cheddar cheese
2 lbs. ground sausage
5 eggs
2 1/4 c. milk
1/2 tsp. dry mustard
1 can cream of mushroom soup
1/2 c. milk
1/4 c. red and green peppers, chopped

Grease a 9" x 13" baking dish. Brown sausage and drain. Set aside. Place bread cubes over bottom of dish. Sprinkle with the cheese. Place sausage on top of cheese. Beat eggs with 2 1/4 cups milk and mustard. Pour over the sausage. Cover and refrigerate the casserole overnight. In the morning, dilute the soup with the 1/2 cup of milk and pour over casserole. Sprinkle with chopped peppers. Bake at 325 for 30-35 minutes.

FRUIT TREE

- *A natural and nutritious table decoration.*

Purchase a spiked wooden form from your local craft supply store (or make your own using a wooden cone with nails as spikes). Press fresh fruits of all kinds onto the spikes. Try using pomegranates, lemons, limes, apples, kumquats, oranges, etc. A small pineapple on the top looks nice. Tuck sprigs of greenery in between the fruits to act as a filler. Small bunches of grapes may also be used to fill in spaces. This makes a very attractive centerpiece and can be casual or elegant.

106

CANDY CANE BRITTLE

- *Use crushed candy canes instead of peanuts in this holiday brittle.*

  1 c. granulated sugar
  1/2 c. light corn syrup
  2 Tbs. water
  1 Tbs. butter
  1/8 tsp. salt
  1 tsp. baking soda
  1/2 c. coarsely crushed peppermint candy canes

Mix sugar, corn syrup, and water in a heavy saucepan. Stirring constantly, bring to a boil over medium heat. Cook until hard crack stage (300 degrees) or until mixture becomes light brown. A small amount of syrup in cold water will form brittle threads when mixture is done. Remove from heat and add butter and salt. When butter has melted stir in soda (mixture will foam). Spread candy cane pieces on a greased cookie sheet or greased aluminum foil. Pour syrup over the candy. Cool and break into pieces. Store in an airtight container.

To make a **peppermint brittle wreath,** generously grease a 12" pizza pan and the outside of a small heatproof bowl or custard cup. Place the bowl upside down in the center of the pizza pan. Sprinkle candy cane pieces on the pizza pan. Pour the syrup around the bowl onto the pizza pan. Let cool and carefully remove bowl. For a gift, wrap wreath in plastic wrap or cellophane and add a bow.

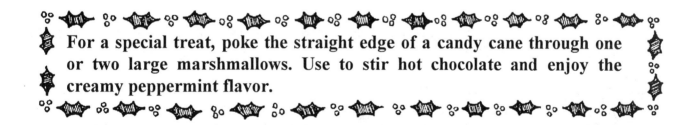

For a special treat, poke the straight edge of a candy cane through one or two large marshmallows. Use to stir hot chocolate and enjoy the creamy peppermint flavor.

EDIBLE POINSETTIAS

- *Decorate cakes or cupcakes with these holiday flowers.*

Using red fruit leather rolls, cut poinsettia-shaped leaves with kitchen shears. Cut 5-7 red leaves. Arrange on cake as a flower. Place 3-5 small yellow candies in the center, securing with icing if needed. Green leaves can be made by rolling soft green spearmint candies or gumdrops onto a granulated sugared surface. Cut into a leaf shape and place under red poinsettia leaves. Pretty and edible!

GRANDMA'S COOKIE CLUB

- *Grandchildren will remember this gift for years to come.*

A clever gift for a grandmother to give to a grandchild of any age. "Enroll" each child in Grandma's cookie-of-the-month club. Each month bake and take (or send) a box full of cookies to the grandchild. You will get rave reviews! This would be great for a birthday gift and subsequent cookies could be sent each month on the date that corresponds to the child's birth.

CHOCOLATE SNOWBALLS

- *A bite-sized treat that will melt-in-your-mouth.*

> 1 large (7 oz.) chocolate bar
> 1 container (8 oz.) whipped topping
> Crushed vanilla wafers or flaked coconut

Melt the chocolate bar in a double boiler. Cool slightly and fold in whipped topping. Make spoon-sized balls and roll into finely crushed vanilla wafers or flaked coconut. Freeze or refrigerate until ready to serve.

TORTILLA SNOWFLAKES

- *Hang these yummy ornaments on your tree and the decorations may not last long!*

Place a flour tortilla on a cutting board. Using miniature cookie cutters or scissors, cut shapes out of the tortilla and edges so it resembles a snowflake. Place on a baking sheet and brush with melted margarine. Bake at 375 degrees for 4-6 minutes or until tortilla is golden brown. Sprinkle with powdered sugar.

DRESS UP YOUR PUNCH BOWL

- *Add holiday finery to your punch.*

Make a festive punch bowl by trying some of the following ideas. Freeze maraschino cherries in ice cubes or an ice ring and float in punch. Sprigs of mint are also attractive floating in the punch. To avoid diluting punch, make ice cubes out of lemon-lime soda or lemon juice. Another unique idea for a Christmas punch bowl is to secure a clean, tall, red or green candle in the bottom of the punch bowl with candle wax, and serve the punch from around the candle.

COOKIE STACKS

- *Send a stack of cookies home with your dinner guests.*

Make your favorite sugar cookie dough. Using a cookie cutter, cut a holiday shape from the dough. A simple shape such as a bell, star, or tree works best. Make cookies the same size or graduate cookie shapes from small to large. Bake cookies and let cool. Do not frost with icing. Colored sugars sprinkled on top before baking or immediately after coming out of the oven add a nice festive touch. Stack cookies on top of each other 8-10 high. Place a paper doily in between each cookie. Tie a holiday ribbon around cookies like a gift. Tie a bow on top.

GINGERBREAD COOKIE ORNAMENTS

- *A delicious and inexpensive way to decorate your tree.*

2/3 c. margarine	1 tsp. baking soda
1/2 c. granulated sugar	1 tsp. salt
1/2 c. brown sugar	1 tsp. ginger
1 egg	1 tsp. cinnamon
1/4 c. molasses	1 tsp. cloves
2 c. flour	

Cream together margarine, granulated sugar, and brown sugar. Add egg, molasses, soda, salt, and spices. Stir in flour and mix well. Roll out onto a floured surface and using Christmas cookie cutters, cut shapes. Place cookies onto a greased cookie sheet and bake at 375 degrees for 10 minutes. Immediately after removing cookies from oven, press a drinking straw through the top of each cookie to make a hole. Make sure hole is at least 1/2" from the edge. String each cookie ornament with ribbon or jute for hanging. Plaid ribbon looks nice with plain cookies. Decorate cookies with Royal Icing (see page 102), if desired, or add details with acrylic paint for non-edible cookie ornaments.

To make a **gingerbread bowl**, make gingerbread cookie dough as above. Roll the dough out large enough to shape around the outside of an oven safe bowl (a 1 or 2 quart bowl will work best). Lightly grease the outside of the bowl and shape dough around bowl. Cut small shapes from the top edge using a small cookie cutter or a knife. Shapes such as hearts, stars, and small trees look nice. Place bowl upside down onto a cookie sheet. Bake at 325 degrees for 25-30 minutes. Remove from oven and let cool. Remove gingerbread from bowl. Use to serve candy or fill with cookies.

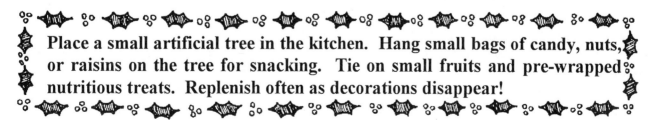

Place a small artificial tree in the kitchen. Hang small bags of candy, nuts, or raisins on the tree for snacking. Tie on small fruits and pre-wrapped nutritious treats. Replenish often as decorations disappear!

CANDIED SPOON STIRRERS

- *Add an extra special flavor to your hot spiced holiday drinks.*

Place stainless steel spoons or heavyweight clear plastic spoons on a cookie sheet lined with waxed paper. Make sure spoon handles are on the rim of the cookie sheet so the spoons are level.

Make your favorite hard candy lollipop recipe (or use recipe below). Before adding flavor and color, divide syrup into several heat proof bowls. Add a different flavor and color to each. Some nice combinations to try are orange coloring with orange flavoring, yellow with lemon, red with cinnamon or cherry, and green with lime. Gently pour a small amount of syrup into each spoon on the cookie sheet. Allow the candy to harden. You now have spoons filled with hard candy of different colors and flavors. (Crushed hard candies can also be used. Just add a few drops of light corn syrup and melt over low heat.) If plastic spoons are used, make sure to use heavy-duty plastic and let candy syrup cool slightly before pouring into spoons to prevent spoons from melting.

For a nice gift, fill a jar with different colored candy spoons and add directions for use. Use to stir hot spiced drinks. These are great for hot wassail and add an extra tang to the drink. Fun for a party!

LOLLIPOPS

- *A basic recipe for making colorful lollipops.*

> 1 c. granulated sugar
> 1/3 c. light corn syrup
> 1/2 c. water
> 1/2 tsp. oil flavoring
> Food coloring

Combine the first three ingredients in a heavy saucepan. Cook over medium heat and stir to dissolve sugar. Bring to a boil. Boil until mixture reaches 300 degrees (hard crack stage) on a candy thermometer. Remove from heat and add flavoring and food coloring. Pour candy into metal lollipop molds with sticks inserted (molds available at craft and candy making supply stores). When cool, remove from molds. Place each lollipop in a small plastic lollipop bag or wrap with plastic wrap. Tie curling ribbon around each bag to close. Makes 12-15 lollipops.

SUGAR SYRUP SNOWFLAKES

- *Drizzle colorful candy syrup to make one-of-a-kind "snowflake" ornaments.*

Grease a cookie sheet. Draw 4" circles onto the greased cookie sheet to use as a guide. Make the lollipop recipe (above) and with a spoon, drizzle the hot prepared lollipop syrup randomly onto the circles. Use a back and forth motion, staying within the circles, to create lacy looking candy "snowflakes." Let harden and gently remove with a spatula. Thread a ribbon through one of the openings in each candy snowflake and use as ornaments or as holiday treats. Store in a cool, dry place.

LOLLIPOP TREE

- *A "sweet" gift for all ages.*

To make a lollipop tree holder, cut a 1" dowel 6" in length. Cut a 1" x 4" x 4" piece of pine board and nail or screw dowel to the middle of the square. Spray paint entire tree green or paint with acrylic paint. Drill 13 holes the diameter of the lollipop sticks approximately 1/2" deep into the dowel. Drill one hole on top of the dowel and alternate the other 12 on the sides of the dowel. Make sure to drill holes on an angle so lollipops won't fall out. Wire a holiday bow around the base of tree. Insert wrapped lollipops into the drilled holes. A variety of different colored and flavored lollipops look nice although one batch of a single color and flavor will fill one tree. (See Lollipop recipe, page 110.) Add a gift tag. A lollipop tree makes a perfect gift for a neighbor, co-worker, or a teacher.

GINGERBREAD MIX

- *Make baking easy for your friends.*

Mix the dry ingredients of a gingerbread cookie recipe together. Package mix in a jar or a fabric bag. For a gift, include a recipe with instructions for adding wet ingredients to the mix. Attach gingerbread men cookie cutters and you have a quick and inexpensive gift!

HOLIDAY HUNT

- *A gift wrapped treasure hunt.*

Create a treasure hunt by wrapping each clue in a small package. Treasures that can be shared with everyone, such as cookies, are best. You may wish to try this Christmas morning with the treasure being a family gift from Santa.

PERSONALIZED PLACEMATS

- *These placemats make a great gift for a shut-in or a far away friend.*

Purchase a supply of inexpensive paper placemats. (Paper placemats come in a variety of colors and can be purchased at a party supply store.) Decorate each placemat with cartoons, jokes, or pictures cut from newspapers or magazines. Personalized drawings can also be used and placemats can be dated if desired. Give as a gift and the recipient can use a different placemat each day and enjoy the creativity.

CHRISTMAS ADVENT BASKET

- *This basket of gifts is especially nice for the sick and lonely.*

Wrap 25 small gifts, one to open each day of December. Gifts can be numbered from one to twenty-five if desired. Gifts can include pencils, candy bars, seed packages, holiday napkins, notebooks, recipe cards, canned foods, puzzles, books, soap, lotion, stickers, etc. Choose gifts that would be appropriate for the person receiving the gifts. Wrap each gift and place in a pretty basket or other holiday container. This advent basket gives the recipient something special to look forward to each day until Christmas.

HOLIDAY PILLOWCASES

- *A great gift for grandmother to make for grandchildren.*

Children as well as adults will enjoy sleeping on a holiday pillowcase. They are simple to make. Measure one of your pillowcases at home and purchase that amount of fabric plus a little extra to turn under for the hem and seams. There are wonderful fabrics available for every holiday. Make a pillowcase for each holiday throughout the year!

REINDEER TAGS

- *A fun way to keep the recipient of a gift secret until Christmas morning.*

To help keep packages under the tree from being "peeked" at or just to help create a little suspense, try this idea. Assign each member of your family a reindeer name (Rudolph, Dancer, Prancer, etc.) that only you know the identity of. Label all packages for each person with their "reindeer name." Family members will have a lot of fun trying to determine which packages belong to them. On Christmas morning reveal the "reindeer names" and enjoy the fun!

HANDPRINT GIFTS

- *Make a memory gift.*

Purchase or make a tablecloth, pillow, pillowcase, or apron. Pour acrylic paints mixed with fabric medium onto a plate. Have your child press hands in the paint and carefully place hands onto project to be decorated. Use a permanent marker for signing names next to handprints. When the paint dries, iron the project to help set the paint permanently. A project like this will make a special gift for a teacher or a grandparent.

GIFT WRAPPED CANDY BARS

- *Keep some of these on hand for when you need a quick gift.*

Purchase large or small candy bars that are wrapped with gold or silver foil under the paper label. Remove the paper label to use as a pattern. Lay the label on holiday wrapping paper and cut a piece the same size. Wrap the holiday paper around the candy bar replacing the original outside wrapper so the foil is showing on each end. Use a glue stick to glue paper where it overlaps on the back of the candy bar. Decorate with stickers or small bows. A nice stocking stuffer!

ADVENT STORY BOOK

- *Read a holiday story each night until Christmas Eve. A nice tradition to start.*

Gather 24 Christmas stories or poems. Find stories that have meaning to your family and portray the spirit of the holidays. You may wish to use stories from your life or your ancestors' lives. Type each story on a separate page and have it spiral bound at a copy center for a keepsake. Starting December 1st, read one story each night. Christmas Eve end by reading the story of the Nativity found in the Bible.

PUZZLE WREATH

- *Recycle old cardboard puzzles by making fun decorations.*

Cut a cardboard circle the size you want your wreath to be. Cut the center of the cardboard out leaving a 2" wide ring. Using an old puzzle, lay the pieces on newspaper and spray paint green. Let dry. Glue puzzle pieces on the cardboard ring with craft glue. Add several layers of puzzle pieces placing them randomly so the cardboard ring is covered. Add a bow and glue some red pom-poms around the wreath to resemble holly berries. Hang with craft wire. This is a great project for children. *Note:* If you don't have an old puzzle, use wadded up balls of newsprint and glue onto the cardboard ring. Spray entire wreath with green spray paint and add a bow.

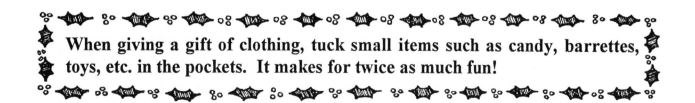

When giving a gift of clothing, tuck small items such as candy, barrettes, toys, etc. in the pockets. It makes for twice as much fun!

CHRISTMAS DOORS

- *Proudly display your child's art.*

A great place to hang your children's art work is on their bedroom doors. This will give children a place to proudly display their holiday creations. If children share a bedroom, assign a another door in the house to decorate such as the closet, bathroom, basement, or family room door.

GIFT WRAPPED WALLS

- *A creative way to decorate your walls for the holidays.*

Choose some attractive holiday wrapping paper. Take down the pictures you have on your walls and wrap them as you would a gift. Tie with wide ribbon and add large bows. Hang the pictures back on the wall. Your walls will now be covered with "packages." Gift tags also add an extra special touch.

GUEST GUESS

- *Have holiday visitors try their luck at guessing the number of candies in a jar.*

Fill a large jar or container with holiday candies. You might try candy canes, taffy, small candy bars, chocolate kisses, gumdrops, etc. Add a bow on top and place next to your front door or somewhere it can easily be seen. As friends, family, and neighbors come to your home throughout the holidays, have them make a guess as to how many pieces of candy are in the jar. Keep paper and a pencil, nearby to record names and guesses. Place in a small box or container until the end of the contest.

On a designated day, possibly the morning of Christmas Eve, read the guesses and determine which guess was the closest to the actual number of candies in the jar. Deliver the jar of candies to the lucky winner! (Don't forget to sing a Christmas carol.) This is a fun tradition everyone, especially children, will look forward to for years to come.

"ABC" CHRISTMAS CARD BOOK

- *Recycled Christmas cards provide a learning experience.*

Make a book using approximately 14 sheets of white or colored cardstock or paper. Tie pages together with yarn or staple along the edge. Have a child color the cover. Inside, label each side of the page with a letter of the alphabet. Have available Christmas cards, toy catalogs, or printed wrapping paper, scissors, and glue. The child must cut an item out of a card, toy catalog, or wrapping paper and glue it to the page with the letter of the alphabet in which the item starts. This helps children learn their alphabet, and also allows them to enjoy creating their own special holiday book.

114

WRAP IT UP

- *Be creative with your holiday gift wrap.*

Gifts can be wrapped with many different things and personalized for the recipient. Something out of the ordinary can be fun and save money as well. Try some of the following:

Newsprint (comics are great for kids)
Posters
Fabric
Cellophane
Sheet music (wrap tapes and cd's)
Children's artwork
Wallpaper
Road maps
Decorated paper sacks
Christmas tablecloths (paper or cloth)

Try sponge-painting, stamping, stencilling, or letting your children draw on lengths of plain newsprint (available for a minimal cost from a newspaper printer), butcher, or kraft paper. Grandparents especially love the artwork of their grandchildren. Children's hands brushed with acrylic paint and pressed firmly on the paper to make handprints makes a great wrap. Be creative and have fun!

A simple tip to find the correct amount of wrapping paper needed to wrap a gift, is to wrap a string around the package and cut it to use as a guide to measure the paper. Don't forget that ribbon can be recycled by ironing it to make it look like new.

GLITTER STARS

- *Add glitter to your presents and sparkle to your tree.*

To make glitter star ornaments you will need assorted colors of glitter, waxed paper, and white craft glue. Draw stars on the waxed paper with glue, using the pointed tip of the glue bottle to help shape it. Generously sprinkle glitter over the glue, making sure it is completely covered. Shake off excess glitter. Let the stars dry 4-5 hours. Carefully peel the waxed paper away, working in from each point. Glitter stars make great Christmas tree ornaments or package decorations. They are easy to make and you can turn out dozens of them in a short time. A great inexpensive holiday project.

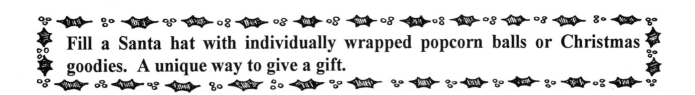

Fill a Santa hat with individually wrapped popcorn balls or Christmas goodies. A unique way to give a gift.

HOMEMADE FINGER PAINT AND CLAY

- *Great gifts from Grandma!*

FINGER PAINT
    3 Tbs. granulated sugar
    1/2 c. cornstarch
    2 c. cold water
    Food coloring

Place sugar, cornstarch, and water in a saucepan. Cook over medium heat stirring constantly until well blended and thick. Divide mixture into 4 portions and add different food coloring to each. This will dry out easily so store in jars with tight lids or use immediately.

BATHTUB FINGER PAINT
    1/3 c. cornstarch
    1 1/2 c. water
    3 Tbs. talcum powder
    3 Tbs. mild liquid dishwashing soap
    Food coloring

Stir together cornstarch and add water a little at a time in a heavy saucepan. Blend well. Stirring continuously over medium heat, cook until mixture comes to a boil and thickens. Remove from heat and add the talcum powder and dishwashing soap. Stir well. Divide mixture into portions and add several drops of a different food coloring to each. Mix well. Store in small, covered containers until ready to use. Let children "paint" in the bathtub!

CLAY
    1 c. cornstarch
    1 1/4 c. cold water
    1 c. baking soda

Blend soda, cornstarch, and water. Stir until smooth. Cook over medium heat until mixture boils. Continue to cook and stir until mixture looks like mashed potatoes. Cover and cool in refrigerator for 1/2 hour. Knead well. Add a few drops of water if clay is dry. Store in a plastic bag in the refrigerator. Left out, this clay will harden so it can be painted.

116

SALT DOUGH ORNAMENTS

- *Create one-of-a-kind ornaments.*

    2 c. flour
    1 c. salt
    1 c. water

In a large bowl combine flour and salt and mix well. Slowly add water and mix until a ball forms. If the dough becomes too sticky add a little more flour.

Knead dough for about 10 minutes until firm and smooth. Place dough in a plastic bag and refrigerate until ready to use. If it's too dry when you remove it from the refrigerator, sprinkle with water.

To make ornaments, roll dough to about 1/4" thick. Using greased cookie cutters, cut shapes from the dough. Add textures to the surface of the shapes by using toothpicks, forks, spoons, garlic presses, graters, etc. When adding one piece of dough to another, moisten both edges with water and press together. Make a hole at the top of the ornament for hanging.

Ornaments can be air dried or baked. To air dry, place on a screen tray and place in a warm area. To bake, place ornaments on a foil covered cookie sheet and place in a 325 degree oven. Bake for about 1/2 hour. Watch them close and reduce heat if they brown too quickly. Baking may cause them to be puffy. Air dried ornaments will have a flatter shape than the baked ones.

Paint the dried ornaments with acrylic paints. Allow the paint to dry thoroughly and seal with spray varnish or shellac to protect against humidity.

GIFT EXCHANGE GAME

- *Want a fun way to exchange gifts at a party? Try this.*

For a fun game at a Christmas party, have each guest bring a wrapped gift. When it is time to exchange the gifts, instruct guests to sit in a circle and hold a gift on their lap. It does not matter if they are holding the same gift they brought to the party.

To play, the host or hostess reads a statement and the guests follow the instructions to exchange their gifts. For example, if the host states "everyone who is wearing red exchange" then all guests with red clothing must stand and switch gifts with someone else who is standing. (If you have a small group, gifts may be exchanged with anyone standing, or if a large group, you may want gifts passed to the person standing on the right.) Continue until everyone has switched their gifts at least several times.

Ideas for exchange statements:

Everyone who…exchange gifts.

is wearing red	has two Christmas trees
has a hole in his/her sock	has their stockings hung
has pierced ears	has been caroling this year
likes eggnog	is going out of town this month
has ridden in a sleigh	is wearing green
has a birthday in December	has a red or green car
has brown hair	has built a snowman this year
has green eyes	has baked Christmas cookies
is wearing nail polish	is wearing a necklace
has been to the North Pole	has a nose like a cherry
has their holiday shopping finished	has Christmas lights on their house
wears glasses	is wearing a watch
has mistletoe in their home	likes fruitcake

CHRISTMAS SOUNDS

- *Try to recognize recorded holiday sounds. A great party game!*

Using a tape recorder, record sounds around your home that are associated with Christmas. Examples of sounds you may wish to include are bells ringing, a present being unwrapped, a fire crackling, popcorn popping, etc. Make some easy and some harder. Give each person a piece of paper and a pencil. Play the recording and give a prize to the person who guesses the most sounds correctly.

GIFT EXCHANGE STORY

- *This fast-paced gift exchange game will create lots of laughter!*

Have each guest bring a wrapped gift for the gift exchange. Everyone sits in a circle while a narrator reads the following story, "A Christmas Eve To Remember." Each time the words **left, right,** or **Wright** are mentioned, the gifts are passed in that direction. Each person will keep the gift they are holding at the end of the story.

A Christmas Eve To Remember

It was a beautiful Christmas Eve. The snow was falling. Everything seemed perfectly **right** for the evening. There was enough hot chocolate **left** to share with Santa, **right** along with the plate of cookies **left** for him by the fireplace.

Ed and Myrna **Wright** thought it would be a great time to drive across town and deliver Grandmother **Wright's** Christmas gift. Grandmother **Wright** had not **left** her home for a week. She was **right** down in bed, as the flu had **left** her feeling weak.

Mr. **Wright** and Mrs. **Wright left** in their bright red car. They had just turned **left** out of the driveway when Mrs. **Wright** said to Mr. **Wright,** "I **left** Grandmother's present **right** there on the kitchen counter." Mr. **Wright** quickly turned **right** back into the driveway and Mrs. **Wright** leaned **left** as he did so. She hopped **right** out of the car and **left** her door open. Mrs. **Wright** said, "I will be **right** back." Snowball, their dog, saw the door open and jumped **right** into the car, **right** over the front seat and **right** into the back seat. About this time, Mrs. **Wright** showed up with Grandmother's present and said to Mr. **Wright,** "It was **right** where I **left** it, in the kitchen."

Mrs. **Wright** was surprised to see Snowball in the car. Mrs. **Wright** thought they had **left** him in the back yard. However, Mr. **Wright** had forgotten and **left** the gate unlocked. Mr. and Mrs. **Wright left** Snowball in the back seat of the car as they once again **left** their driveway for Grandmother **Wright's** home. As Mr. and Mrs. **Wright** drove along enjoying the beautiful scenery they felt as if they had **left** all their worries somewhere else.

It was Christmas Eve and they were surrounded, both on the **right** and on the **left** with new falling snow. They were getting that wonderful feeling that often comes at Christmas time.

(continued)

Mr. **Wright's** car turned **right** onto Holly street where Grandmother **Wright** lived. As they approached Grandmother **Wright's** they could see she had **left** her porch light on. It felt **right** chilly when they stepped out of the car. However, they **left** their jackets in the car. Mr. **Wright** and Mrs. **Wright** were glad they had not **left** Grandmother **Wright's** gift home. They could see Grandmother **Wright** peeking through the curtains as they walked up her steps. Snowball began to bark as he did not want to be **left** out. What a nice surprise for Grandmother **Wright,** she had not been **left** alone on Christmas Eve. Mr. **Wright** and Mrs. **Wright** walked **right** up to the door and knocked. Grandmother **Wright,** stood **right** by the door and opened it **right** as soon as they knocked. It almost **left** them speechless to see Grandmother **Wright** up and about. Grandmother **Wright** said, "What a wonderful surprise." Mr. **Wright** and Mrs. **Wright** were also surprised to see that Grandmother **Wright** had **left** her bed. She was **right** spry and it was easy to see that her illness had not **left** her weak.

Grandmother **Wright** wanted to celebrate what was **left** of Christmas Eve. So Grandmother **Wright left** Mr. **Wright** and Mrs. **Wright** and went **right** into the kitchen to stir up a pot of hot wassail. She said, "I need my glasses to see this festive recipe, and they are not **right** here where I **left** them." The three of them **left** the kitchen and looked in other rooms to see where she had **left** them. Grandmother **Wright** yelled out, "Well here they are, **right** here where I **left** them." Sure enough they were **right** there on her night stand where she had **left** them.

Grandmother **Wright** made sure she had all the **right** ingredients in the hot wassail. Mr. **Wright** built a fire in the fireplace and it **left** a warm festive feeling as they set on the cozy stuffed sofa, listening to soft Christmas music and sipping their wassail, which was just the **right** temperature. Mr. **Wright** opened the door to check on Snowball and he was fast asleep, **right** there on the doorstep where they had **left** him. Mr. **Wright** and Mrs. **Wright** will never forget this special evening as they were **left** with the true spirit of Christmas in their hearts, and they knew they had done the **right** thing by sharing their Christmas Eve with Grandmother **Wright.**

LUMINARIA LIGHTS

- *Invite your neighborhood to light up the night!*

Duplicate the opposite page *"NEIGHBORHOOD LUMINARIA NIGHT"* onto bright green or red paper and give to your neighbors several weeks before the luminaria night. A reminder may need to be passed out the night before so everyone can be prepared. (You may wish to purchase small brown paper sacks and tea-light candles for each neighbor as your gift to them.) A great tradition to start.

CHRISTMAS SCAVENGER HUNT

- *The first team to collect certain Christmas items wins. Great for teenagers.*

You will need two teams of people for a scavenger hunt. The more the merrier! Give each team a list of items they must collect (one item per house visited) within a certain allotted time. Twenty items in 30 minutes usually works well. Give each team lists with the same items or different lists. Make sure to add some easy items as well as some that will be more difficult to find. Meet back for refreshments, and the team that has collected the most items from its list wins.

Suggested items to collect:

ornament	peanut brittle	pinecone	candy cane
angel	mistletoe	cranberry	Christmas card
jingle bell	cookie	snowball	gift bow
light bulb	mittens	fire log	gingerbread man
a Santa	an elf	star	gift tag
candle	scarf	popcorn ball	poinsettia
gumdrop	wreath	wrapped package	pine bough
snowflake	holly	stocking	ice skate
ear muffs	tinsel	fruitcake	ski pole

CANDY SLEIGH RACE

- *A chocolate Santa rides a candy sleigh to the finish line!*

Divide party guests into several teams or let each person play as an individual. Give each team or player a large candy bar, two candy canes, a chocolate foil-wrapped Santa, and a roll of clear tape. Instruct them to make a sled using the items. When finished, have the teams "race" their sleds by sliding them down a ramp. Make a ramp by using a piece of plywood or a card table propped up on a chair. Cover with butcher paper to make smooth. Have several rounds and then determine the winner by elimination. Let everyone eat their creations!

NEIGHBORHOOD LUMINARIA NIGHT

DATE: _____
6:00 - 8:00 p.m.

LIGHT UP OUR NEIGHBORHOOD WITH *LUMINARIA!*

LUMINARIA ARE PAPER LANTERNS THAT LINE YOUR DRIVEWAY AND SIDEWALKS. THEY ARE SIMPLE AND FUN TO MAKE!

YOU WILL NEED: BROWN OR WHITE PAPER LUNCH BAGS
SAND OR ROCK SALT
VOTIVE OR TEA-LIGHT CANDLES

DIRECTIONS:

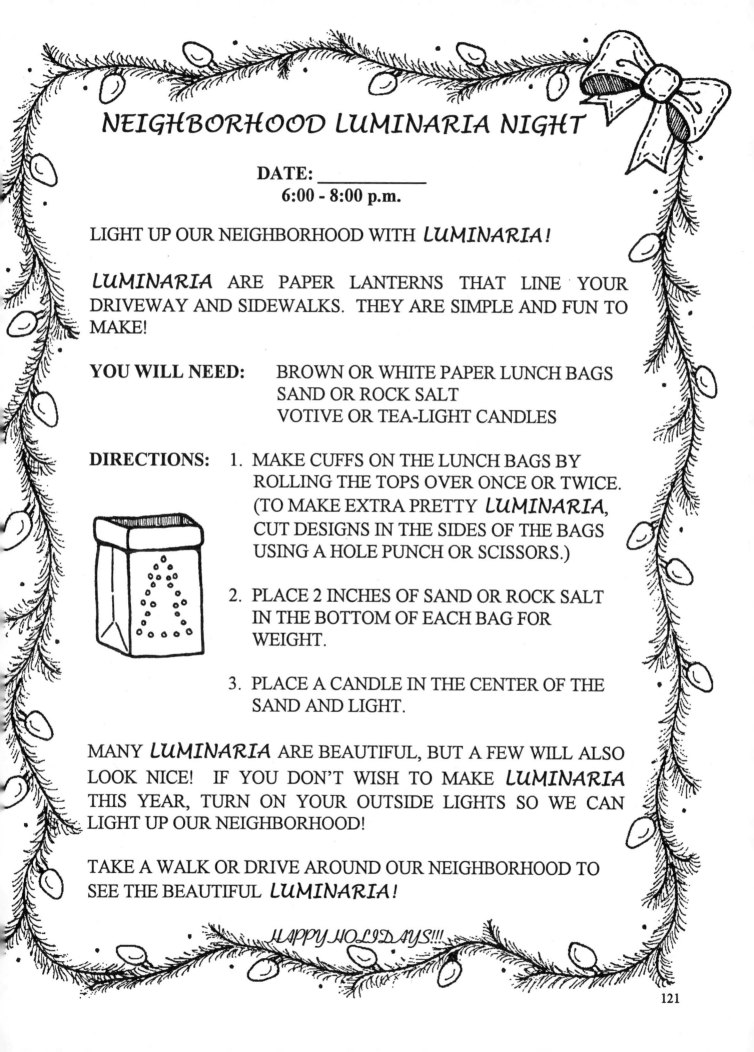

1. MAKE CUFFS ON THE LUNCH BAGS BY ROLLING THE TOPS OVER ONCE OR TWICE. (TO MAKE EXTRA PRETTY *LUMINARIA*, CUT DESIGNS IN THE SIDES OF THE BAGS USING A HOLE PUNCH OR SCISSORS.)

2. PLACE 2 INCHES OF SAND OR ROCK SALT IN THE BOTTOM OF EACH BAG FOR WEIGHT.

3. PLACE A CANDLE IN THE CENTER OF THE SAND AND LIGHT.

MANY *LUMINARIA* ARE BEAUTIFUL, BUT A FEW WILL ALSO LOOK NICE! IF YOU DON'T WISH TO MAKE *LUMINARIA* THIS YEAR, TURN ON YOUR OUTSIDE LIGHTS SO WE CAN LIGHT UP OUR NEIGHBORHOOD!

TAKE A WALK OR DRIVE AROUND OUR NEIGHBORHOOD TO SEE THE BEAUTIFUL *LUMINARIA!*

HAPPY HOLIDAYS!!!

HOLIDAY FUN

- *Christmas activities to make your holidays merry.*

Snow Art
Fill squirt guns or spray bottles with colored water. Color the water by adding food coloring. Children will have hours of fun squirting colored designs onto the snow.

Holiday Slumber Party
Sleep one night around the Christmas tree in sleeping bags. This would be fun the night before Christmas Eve. Adults, children, and grandchildren will all cherish this time together. Tell Christmas stories and play soft Christmas music as you enjoy the lights on the tree.

Santa's Workshop
Children will love this treasure hunt. Give each child a Christmas stocking or a paper sack. Tell the children they are in Santa's workshop, and they must gather all sorts of goodies for Santa's trip on Christmas Eve. The children must find the gifts hidden around the house or room. What they find they may keep. To prepare for the treasure hunt, you will need to wrap small gifts in Christmas paper and hide them. Items such as pencils, lollipops, peanuts, candy canes, play money, little metal cars, gumdrops, pencil sharpeners, trinkets, costume jewelry, crayons, or bubbles can be hidden. Have enough so that even the small children can find their share.

Clap-a-Carol
This game is especially fun for teenagers and adults. It can be played with a small or large group. One person is selected to clap out a well known Christmas carol. The first person who identifies the carol gets a turn to then clap out another carol while the group once again tries to guess.

Pin the Tail on the Reindeer
This game is played the same way as pin the tail on the donkey except that the tail is pinned on the reindeer. You will need one large picture of a reindeer to tape on the wall. Give everyone a cut-out tail with a piece of tape on the back. Take turns blindfolding each person, spin them around, and aim them towards the reindeer. The person must tape the tail to the first place that is touched. The tail that is nearest to the correct spot is the winner. Other games played the same way could include pin the star over Bethlehem, pin the nose on Rudolph, pin the star on the top of the tree, pin the sock on the fireplace, etc.

Christmas Word Scramble
Give each player a list of words relating to Christmas and see who can be the first to unscramble them. Here are some words you may use:

onetatisip	(poinsettia)	erte	(tree)
gmearn	(manger)	ylohl	(holly)
stgif	(gifts)	gisehl	(sleigh)
ttsuhcesn	(chestnuts)	mhhbeetle	(Bethlehem)
rmsihscta	(Christmas)	deehhssrp	(shepherds)
ieeerrnd	(reindeer)	ysot	(toys)
sasalwi	(wassail)	tteelmios	(mistletoe)
luye	(yule)	snteli	(tinsel)
necnepoi	(pinecone)	gneal	(angel)

MERRY CHISTMAS CAROLS

- *How well do you know your holiday carols? This game will test your memory.*

The following are lines or phrases from well known Christmas songs. Give a prize to the person who can guess the most song titles.

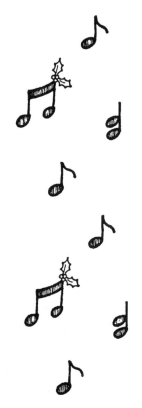

1. …decorations of red on a green Christmas tree… (Blue Christmas)
2. …bring us some figgy pudding… (We Wish You A Merry Christmas)
3. …where the tree tops glisten… (White Christmas)
4. …tidings of comfort and joy… (God Rest Ye Merry Gentlemen)
5. …joyful, all ye nations rise… (Hark the Herald Angels Sing)
6. …strike the harp and join the chorus… (Deck the Halls)
7. …not only green when summer's here… (O Christmas Tree)
8. …star with royal beauty bright… (We Three Kings)
9. …to the earth it gave great light… (The First Noel)
10. …above thy deep and dreamless sleep… (O Little Town of Bethlehem)
11. …the jingle hop has begun… (Jingle-Bell Rock)
12. …our cheeks are nice and rosy… (Sleigh Ride)
13. …then one foggy Christmas Eve… (Rudolph the Red-Nosed Reindeer)
14. …hear the angel voices… (O Holy Night)
15. …better not pout… (Santa Claus is Comin' to Town)
16. …a new born King to see… (The Little Drummer Boy)
17. …it's the best time of the year… (A Holly Jolly Christmas)
18. …angels bending near the earth… (It Came Upon the Midnight Clear)
19. …let earth receive her king… (Joy to the World)
20. …dressed in a snow-white gown… (Suzy Snowflake)

CREATE A STAMP

- *Quick and inexpensive stamp art.*

Make your own stamps by using a package of comfort insoles used in shoes. Draw a shape onto the insole by using a paper pattern or cut a shape without a pattern. Simple shapes work best.   Glue shape onto a block of wood, fabric side down. Use with a stamp pad or fabric paints.   Stamps can be used to decorate Christmas cards, bookmarks, T-shirts, sweatshirts, stationery, wrapping paper, gift tags, recipe cards, etc. By using your imagination you can create a one-of-a-kind gift.

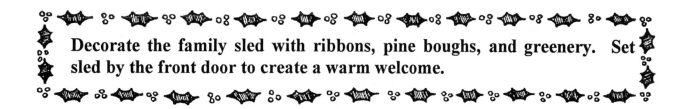

Decorate the family sled with ribbons, pine boughs, and greenery. Set sled by the front door to create a warm welcome.

CHRISTMAS CANDLES

- *Make your holiday bright with candlelight!*

Floating Fruit Candles

Fill a metal bucket or large wash tub with water. Cut a hole the size of a tea-light candle in the top of several red apples. Insert candles in each apple and float in the water. You can also float cranberries and pieces of greenery in the water. Light the candles and place on your porch for a beautiful warm glow.

Canning Jar Candle Holders

To make candle holders for votive or shorter candles, use canning jars of desired size. Paint jar rings either red or green with acrylic paints. Let dry. Screw the rings onto the jars (no lids). This adds some holiday color and pizzazz to the jars. Place candles in the base of the jars using a little melted wax to hold, if necessary. These work great at a dinner table especially with children because the candles are inside the jars and can't be knocked over easily.

Wood Block Candle Holders

Very simple candle holders are made from scraps of wood. Try using blocks of 4" x 4" x 4" pine with a nail in the middle to hold the candle in place. The blocks can be made any size to fit your candles. These are great for candles with a large diameter. Leave the wood natural or wash with a mixture of acrylic paint and water to add just a hint of color. Spray paint gold for an elegant touch.

Apple Candle Holder

Bore a hole in the top of a large red or green apple. Place a taper candle firmly in the hole. Tie a holiday ribbon into a bow where the apple and candle meet.

Fruited Candle Holders

To make beautiful candle holders, try this idea. Scoop out holes the size of votive candles in the tops of oranges, grapefruits, lemons, limes, or pomegranates. Gently twist in votive candles to secure them. (The bottom of each fruit may need to be trimmed to prevent fruits from rocking.) Some juice will seep out around the candles. Sprinkle glitter on top of the fruits and gently shake off the excess. The glitter will stick to the juice and create a lovely accent. Set in groupings inside or out-of-doors.

Frozen Candles

Place candles in the freezer a few hours before using and they will burn slower and more evenly. This will also keep dripping wax to a minimum.

Goblet Candles

Place votive candles into stemmed goblets. Use a variety of goblets and place in groupings at different heights. One-of-a-kind goblets can be purchased inexpensively at yard sales or flea markets.

Cans of Candles

Remove labels from empty cans. Use cans of various sizes such as soup cans, vegetable cans, juice cans, or larger. Wash and dry well. Place a candle in each can making sure it can be seen above the rim. Use large round candles and long taper candles for variety. Set cans in a grouping with greenery intertwined with a garland of miniature lights around the base.

EVERGREEN ICE

- *Beautiful and elegant. These candles will impress even the fussiest guest.*

Iced Beverage Candles

Purchase a bottle of non-alcoholic sparkling cider. Remove labels from the bottle. Open cider and empty into a pitcher. Fully open the top of a clean, empty half-gallon milk carton and place empty bottle inside. Push small cut sprigs of evergreen boughs, cranberries, tinsel, etc. around bottle. Fill carton with water and freeze overnight. When frozen, remove carton by dipping in warm water and peeling the paper away. Using a funnel, pour cider back into bottle. The ice around the bottle will keep the cider cold. Wrap with a clean holiday cloth napkin to serve.

Iced Candles

Place a 2" pillar candle in the center of a clean, empty half-gallon milk carton. Place cut holly or small evergreen boughs around candle. If desired, add cranberries, rose blooms, mistletoe, etc. Fill carton with water leaving top of candle exposed and freeze overnight. When frozen, dip carton in hot water and peel away paper. Set in a small dish to catch the water as ice melts. Arrange greenery at base and use as a centerpiece.

YULETIDE GARLANDS

- *String some of these ideas.*

Using strong thread and a needle, string some of the following items to make a garland:

popcorn	cranberries	cookies
dried apples/fruit	gumdrops	gingerbread
bay leaves	jingle bells	gumballs
beads	wooden spools	buttons
macaroni	lace	cereals

Be creative! Pretzels look pretty strung on a ribbon. Try spraying an old rope with gold spray paint and you have an instant elegant garland. Garlands can add personality and style to a Christmas tree for minimal cost.

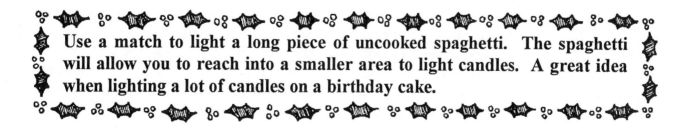

Use a match to light a long piece of uncooked spaghetti. The spaghetti will allow you to reach into a smaller area to light candles. A great idea when lighting a lot of candles on a birthday cake.

FOR THE BIRDS

- *A "tweet" treat.*

Using gingerbread dough, bake and assemble a gingerbread house for the birds to eat. Instead of assembling and decorating with icing, use a mixture of peanut butter, shortening, or suet. Sprinkle the house with birdseed and nuts. More seeds can be added as it is eaten. Depending on where you live, you will have birds, chipmunks, and squirrels feasting on the house.

YULETIDE DECORATIVE SOAP

- *Holiday stickers or small paper motifs adorn this soap.*

Purchase round, oval, or rectangular bar soap. Place a holiday sticker or small paper motif onto the top of the unwrapped soap. To hold sticker or motif on soap, moisten with water. Gently dip the top of the soap into melted paraffin wax, making sure to completely coat the sticker or motif. When soap is used, the sticker or motif will remain in place and will add a nice decorative touch to your home.

HOMEMADE POTPOURRI

- *Enjoy the scents of the season.*

1 dried orange peel
2 dried apple peels
2 1/2 Tbs. whole cloves
1 cinnamon stick

Break the orange and apple peels and the cinnamon stick into small pieces. Simmer in a pot of water to create a lovely holiday fragrance.

PINECONE POTPOURRI

- *These pinecones release a spicy aroma.*

Using a foam craft brush, coat each pinecone with a mixture of 1 part water to 1 part white craft glue. Mix together equal parts of ground cinnamon, ground cloves, and ground ginger. Mix in ground dried orange peel. Sprinkle mixture over the pinecone, coating the glue with the spices. Let dry. Fill a basketful and enjoy!

SNOWBALL TREE

- *Decorate your tree with popcorn balls.*

Make your Christmas tree look like it has been covered with snowballs. Hot glue plain popped popcorn onto a styrofoam ball. Completely cover and let dry. Attach a loop of jute or ribbon to hang. (To make colorful ornaments, use colored popcorn that can be purchased at gourmet food stores.)

PINECONE FIRE STARTERS

- *Keep a basketful of fire starters on the hearth ready for those cold winter nights.*

Supplies needed: Candle wicking
                       Paraffin wax
                       Red crayons
                       Green crayons
                       Muffin tin
                       Medium-sized pinecones (base must fit in a muffin tin)

Pinecones must be dry and fully opened. To open partially closed pinecones, place on a cookie sheet and bake for 30 minutes in a 225 degree oven.

Melt the paraffin wax in a double boiler over low heat. Completely dip each pinecone in the paraffin wax, making sure each is completely coated. Cool on waxed paper. Pour 1/2" of paraffin wax in each cup of a muffin tin. Insert a 2" piece of wick in each muffin cup so it hangs out on the side. Let the paraffin set for several minutes. Press a pinecone into each muffin cup just before the paraffin hardens. Let set until hard.

Dip the bottom of the muffin tin into hot water and gently remove the fire starters. Melt more paraffin as before and add red crayon to color (melt green in another container). Dip the bottoms of the fire starters into red paraffin wax (or green). Repeat a second coat of color if necessary. Let cool on waxed paper. When ready to use, place a fire starter under the kindling and light the wick. Enjoy your cozy fire!

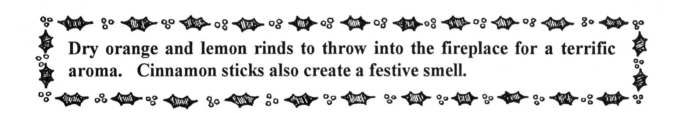

Dry orange and lemon rinds to throw into the fireplace for a terrific aroma. Cinnamon sticks also create a festive smell.

SIMMERING SCENT JAR

- *A fragrant gift idea for a friend or co-worker.*

2 lemon wedges
2 orange slices
1 lime slice
3 Tbs. whole cloves
3 small cinnamon sticks
3 bay leaves

Place ingredients in a glass pint jar. Fill jar with water and place lid and ring on. Decorate lid and attach a small tag with directions for use.

Directions: Place contents of jar in a saucepan. Simmer on stove and add water as needed. Refrigerate to keep fresh.

YULETIDE TABLE SETTING

- *Dress up your table!*

Wreath Place Setting
To decorate a beautiful Christmas table, make a wreath of greenery or pine boughs just large enough for a dinner plate to be set in. Make a wreath by wrapping boughs of greenery together with clear nylon fish line or thin wire so the wreath is flexible. Make one for each place setting. Tie a colorful cloth napkin in a bow and place by each wreath. Using evergreens on your table will not only look beautiful but will create a nice subtle fragrance.

Cookie Cutter Napkin Rings
Use metal cookie cutters as napkin rings. Try shapes such as trees, stars, bells, gingerbread men, etc. Cookie cutters may be spray painted holiday colors if desired. Several coats may be needed.

Exotic Fruit Centerpiece
Fill a basket with exotic fruits such as starfruit, pomegranates, kiwis, breadfruit, papayas, mangos, and kumquats. Many large grocery stores will have a variety to choose from or try a specialty grocer. Use fruit filled basket as a centerpiece or place loose fruit down the center of table with sprigs of greenery and ribbon added. Let each guest take some fruit home. A basket of exotic fruit also makes a great hostess gift.

A Warm Table Setting
Place a large winter scarf down the center of your holiday table and a new mitten at each plate setting. Insert silverware in each mitten.

Jingle Bell Napkin Ring
To make a jingle bell napkin ring, cut a 12" piece of bailing wire or heavy craft wire and string small jingle bells on the wire so they touch. When wire is almost covered, twist the ends together to form a circle large enough to allow napkin to slide through the center. Add a small bow.

Sparkling Fruit Centerpiece
A beautiful non-edible centerpiece can be made by rolling fruit (apples, oranges, pears, pomegranates, etc.) into beaten egg white and then rolling in glitter to coat. Let dry and display fruit in a large bowl or place on a wreath, garland, or mantle.

Quick and Simple Silverware
This simple idea adds a festive holiday touch to a dinner table. Wrap silverware in a cloth or paper napkin and tie with a holiday ribbon. Tie on a jingle bell and place a piece of greenery under the ribbon.

Christmas Card Table Top
Need a place to display Christmas cards? Place them under a glass table top for easy viewing.

Golden Candle Holders
Spray paint small clay pots with gold paint. Place small votive candles inside and group on a mantle or use at each place setting for dinner.

A SPECIAL BIRTHDAY

- *Enjoy a special evening together as a family.*

Christmas is the celebration of the birth of Jesus. Make a birthday cake and choose a time to serve it when your family can be together. Discuss the true meaning of Christmas and what it means to your family. Discuss ways in which your family celebrates the holiday season. This may become a new tradition and will create fond memories.

GIFTS FROM THE HEART

- *Give a gift that can't be purchased.*

Gifts of time often create lasting memories and strengthen family ties. Along with the purchased gifts this year, be sure to make time for a gift of yourself such as reading a story to your child, playing a game, going to the park, or spending time together talking.

WRAPPED NATIVITY

- *A unique way to let everyone participate in the story of the Nativity.*

Wrap each piece of a Nativity set. By wrapping, excitement is added and pieces can be distributed randomly. Pass a wrapped piece to each person and instruct him/her to unwrap it. Select a person to read the story of the Nativity and the visit of the Wisemen found in the Bible. As the person reading the story mentions someone or something represented by a manger piece, the person holding that piece places it in the crèche.

HOLIDAY PROGRESSIVE DINNER

- *Make holiday memories with friends and family.*

If your extended family lives within a reasonable distance of each other, you might try a progressive dinner. This is a great idea for Christmas or New Year's celebrating. Visiting the homes of each relative gives everyone a chance to see and enjoy the decorations and holiday atmosphere of each family's home.

Each family prepares a separate course for the dinner, starting with appetizers and ending with dessert. As each course is finished you move from home to home until all courses have been served. To add to the fun of the evening, everyone could exchange gifts at the conclusion of the dinner.

HOLIDAY HOUSE

- *A reusable "gingerbread house" made from masonite. Decorate this house for Christmas or any other holiday or special occasion.*

To make house:

1. Using the measurements on the pattern as a guide, make paper pattern templates. Trace the templates onto 1/8" masonite.

2. Cut house pieces out of the masonite with a table saw (or other type of saw). Cut all slits 1/8" wide. Lightly sand edges if needed.

3. Lay the two long sides of the roof pieces next to each other. Using clear, 3" wide packaging tape, tape the two roof pieces together. The tape will act as a hinge. (Tape may need to be replaced after several uses.)

Note: House pattern may be enlarged from dimensions given. If enlarging house, use 1/4" masonite. Be sure to cut slits to 1/4" so pieces will fit together.

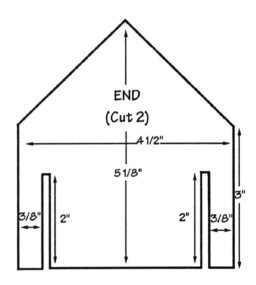

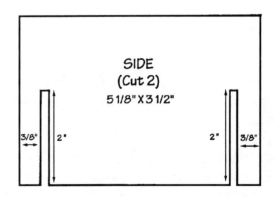

Assembly:

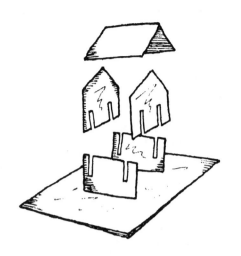

1. Use canned or homemade icing to decorate your holiday house. Royal Icing works best because it hardens as it dries. (Royal Icing can be found on page 102.) Either assemble the house pieces first or decorate each piece and let dry before assembly. If you wish to do the latter, make sure to keep icing away from the grooves so it will fit together easily.

2. Join the front and side pieces by aligning and sliding into the grooves. Place roof on frame of house. You may want to "tack" the house to the base and the roof with icing. (Place a small gift inside the house for an extra clever surprise when giving the house as a gift.)

3. Add candy and decorations as desired. Some suggested decorating ideas are listed below.

To reuse, **gently** hand wash each piece and dry well. You may need to soak the house for a few minutes in hot water to loosen the icing.

DECORATING IDEAS FOR YOUR HOLIDAY HOUSE

New Year's Eve - Tiny clocks, confetti, small plastic baby with diaper, colorful candy sprinkles, party blowers, and noisemakers.

Valentine's Day - Red, white, and pink candies, conversation hearts, peppermints, chocolate kisses, heart-shaped lollipops, candy lips, and cinnamon candies.

St. Patrick's Day - Green candies, shamrocks, gumdrops, gold-foil-wrapped chocolate coins, tiny black pots, rainbows, and plastic leprechauns.

Easter - Pastel colored candies, jelly beans, tinted coconut, marshmallow bunnies, candy eggs, tiny baskets, ribbons, Easter grass, and gumballs.

Fourth of July - Red, white, and blue candies, firecrackers, sparklers, paper or candy stars, and tiny flag picks.

Halloween - Black and orange candies, candy corn, stretchy spider webbing, paper gravestones, plastic ghosts, spiders, cats, bats, skeletons, bugs etc.

Thanksgiving - Candy corn, candy fruits, cornucopias, tiny pilgrims and turkeys, silk leaves, pretzels, dry cereals, crackers, dried fruits, and nuts.

Christmas - Red and green candies, candy canes, gumdrops, a plastic Santa, snowmen, trees, bells, and wreaths. Sprinkle with powdered sugar to create "snow."

Note: There are many wonderful seasonal candies available. Be creative! Shop at your local party supply or craft store for small decorating items.

INDEX

Sweet Surprises For The Holidays

Order Form

Send to:
Gingerbread Garden, LLC
P.O. Box 1213
Centerville, UT 84014-5213

Quantity		**Unit Price**	**Total**
_____	Sweet Surprises for the Holidays	$10.95	_____
	Utah Residents Add 6.25% Tax		_____
	Add $3.00 for shipping & handling (Add $1.00 for each additional book)		_____
		Total	_____

___Check/Money Order   ___Visa   ___M/C

Name _____
        (Print or type)

Account # _____

Expiration Date _____

Signature _____

Name_____

Address_____

City/State/Zip _____

Telephone (opt.)_____-_____